PRAISE FOR
SOMEBODY CARES

Doug Stringer knows what works, for the Lord has given him a blueprint that is transforming the fourth largest city in America and is spreading across the country and the globe. It's time for a marriage of heart-commitment to Jesus with the fulfillment found in unity and servanthood. Doug embodies both, and he shares how it can happen to you and your church, too.

CHÉ AHN
SENIOR PASTOR, HARVEST ROCK CHURCH
PASADENA, CALIFORNIA

Doug Stringer was a city reacher before city reaching was cool. His book tells what happens when the Church is obedient to carry our heavenly Father's heart for our city. If you are ready to do the will of the Father in your city, you need this book.

DANIEL BERNARD
EXECUTIVE DIRECTOR, SOMEBODY CARES TAMPA BAY
TAMPA BAY, FLORIDA

Somebody Cares is a refre   Christians choose to lock hands   orce for reaching out to the peop   Doug Stringer's inspiration and leadership to unity His Body in Houston in order to win people to Christ. What is happening there is truly wonderful and unprecedented and is a model for other cities to follow.

BILL BRIGHT
FOUNDER AND PRESIDENT, CAMPUS CRUSADE FOR CHRIST
ORLANDO, FLORIDA

Scripture tells us our care for and service to others is the measure of true greatness. And that is the testimony of Doug Stringer. To read this book is to know the heart of God and be touched by the Spirit of God.

EDWIN LOUIS COLE
CHRISTIAN MEN'S NETWORK
SOUTHLAKE, TEXAS

Somebody Cares comes from the heart of Doug Stringer, a man who is totally sold out to seeing lives changed by the love of God. His fervency and undaunted tenacity will stir you to stand up and be a witness. I strongly recommend this book to the Body of Christ.

KINGSLEY A. FLETCHER
SENIOR PASTOR, LIFE COMMUNITY CHURCH
RESEARCH TRIANGLE PARK, NORTH CAROLINA

This book contains not only the heart of Doug Stringer but also the heart of the Father for the lost. In this hour, when hopelessness and despair are spread through every avenue of media, this book is a good tonic. *Somebody Cares* doesn't just point the way of hope, it *leads* the way. Read it and be inspired. Behave it and be blessed.

WALTER FLETCHER, JR.
PASTOR OF PRAYER AND ADULT CHRISTIAN EDUCATION, HILLCREST CHURCH
DALLAS, TEXAS

Somebody Cares is not just another evangelistic strategy. It is a reality in the life of Doug Stringer. His book clearly shows how the love of Christ is the only hope we have to make a difference in our cities in this generation. If you want to be a part of something bigger than yourself, if you want to make a difference in this world, you need to read this book. It will change your life!

ROGER L. HELLE
EXECUTIVE DIRECTOR, TEEN CHALLENGE OF THE MID-SOUTH
CHATTANOOGA, TENNESSEE

Doug Stringer lives and writes with an amazing combination of humility and passion. He is not writing from an ivory tower about a theory that sounds good but has no practical relevance. Doug has fought the battles in the trenches. He has sown his life into the lives of men and women from every ethnic and denominational background in the city. The result? God is uniting His Church in Houston, and revival is underway.

JIM HERRINGTON
MISSION HOUSTON
HOUSTON, TEXAS

Doug Stringer has become a leading instrument of harvest in the city of Houston, with a ripple effect reaching out into America and other nations. The heartbeat of his ministry points to the very heart and intentions of God that none should perish.

SCOTT HINKLE
FOUNDER, SCOTT HINKLE OUTREACH MINISTRIES
PHOENIX, ARIZONA

From prayer warriors to church leaders, all will be challenged
by Doug Stringer's revelation of God's purpose to fulfill the destiny
of the Church. His experience and revelation should be
required reading in every school of ministry.

JOHN P. KELLY
EXECUTIVE DIRECTOR, INTERNATIONAL COALITION OF APOSTLES
SOUTHLAKE, TEXAS

As a member of the Houston media, I believe it is very important for
the Body of Christ to be well-informed of the workings of the Holy
Spirit through God's people. Somebody Cares Houston provides such
a vehicle through the dedicated leadership of Doug Stringer, one of
the greatest proponents of Christ-centered unity in our generation.
Somebody Cares is a powerful tool in the hands of Almighty God.

KIMBERLY KOSSIE
COMMUNITY RELATIONS DIRECTOR, KSBJ RADIO
HOUSTON, TEXAS

Doug Stringer is a doer of the Word. His endeavor to reach out to
others is creating relationships with those who are like-minded.
These relationships are establishing a network that is spanning the
United States while gaining the attention of not only the Church
but governmental agencies as well.

HANK MARION
SENIOR PASTOR, BAMMEL BAPTIST CHURCH
HOUSTON, TEXAS

Somebody Cares is about the incredible work of God and how we can participate in His grand design. This is a story of what God does when ordinary people like you and me choose to lay down their own agendas and take God at His Word. It's a call to action from a God of action through a man of action. It's a call to love from the God of love through a man of love. Multitudes are in the valley of decision. They need to see Christ's compassion lived out before them through His Church. The people need to feel His love and acceptance. They need you.

JODIE NELSON
DIRECTOR OF OUTREACH, OPERATION BLESSING INTERNATIONAL
VIRGINIA BEACH, VIRGINIA

Lakewood Church is proud to be part of the Somebody Cares network. Our desire is to cross all denominational, racial and economic lines in an effort to changes lives, and *Somebody Cares* is a textbook of how this is done. Want to change your community? Start acting on the principles in this remarkable book.

JOEL OSTEEN
PASTOR, LAKEWOOD CHURCH
HOUSTON, TEXAS

Doug Stringer understands the correlation between prayer, worship, reconciliation, mercy, ministry and evangelism as few men I know. He literally does the stuff required by God in Isaiah 58 for the healing of a land. Reading his book is like encountering a flame—it will either enlighten and inspire you or burn you with shame and conviction, depending on how it finds you.

JIMMY OWENS
HEAL OUR LAND

Somebody Cares is being lived out in Houston, Texas. God has used Doug Stringer to help the Church see that, together, we can get our arms around a city of any size. Underneath Doug's gentle, humble spirit is a passion for revival that challenges all who hear him to examine their lives and move into all God has for them.

STEVE RIGGLE
PRESIDENT, CHRISTIAN EVANGELISTIC ASSEMBLIES OF CHURCHES
SENIOR PASTOR, GRACE COMMUNITY CHURCH
CLEAR LAKE CITY, TEXAS

This book is absolutely a must read for those who wish to see their city transformed. Doug Stringer speaks with the authority and credibility of someone who lives daily the principles of love and compassion for the needy. Read *Somebody Cares*. It will change you for the better.

ED SILVOSO
PRESIDENT, HARVEST EVANGELISM
SAN JOSE, CALIFORNIA

The message of *Somebody Cares* is the rallying cry of the Holy Spirit to the Bride of Christ today. Doug Stringer is God's mouthpiece to impart this very timely message to the fragmented Body of Christ. The message of the "mended net" should convict all of us to tear apart the barriers that we have built around our churches for so long. Do you want to reap a great harvest of souls? If so, *hear what the Spirit says to the Churches!*

PAUL TAN
PRESIDENT, SOMEBODY CARES SOUTHLAND
SENIOR PASTOR, INTERNATIONAL FULL GOSPEL FELLOWSHIP
CLAREMONT, CALIFORNIA

The spiritual wilderness is crying out for a voice. Doug Stringer is that voice, offering new hope and a vision for reaching the lost that is practical and easily implemented in Houston and cities around the world.

TERRY TEKYL
RENEWAL MINISTRIES
SPRING, TEXAS

God has gifted Doug Stringer to be instrumental in inspiring, unifying and activating the Body of Christ and to be a strategic leader in the coming revival.

JERRY WILES
ASSISTANT VICE PRESIDENT, CHURCH RELATIONS
HOUSTON BAPTIST UNIVERSITY
HOUSTON, TEXAS

A Guide to Living Out Your Faith

somebody
CARES

DOUG STRINGER

Regal

A Division of Gospel Light
Ventura, California, U.S.A.

Published by Regal Books
A Division of Gospel Light
Ventura, California, U.S.A.
Printed in the U.S.A.

Regal Books is a ministry of Gospel Light, an evangelical Christian publisher dedicated to serving the local church. We believe God's vision for Gospel Light is to provide church leaders with biblical, user-friendly materials that will help them evangelize, disciple and minister to children, youth and families.

It is our prayer that this Regal book will help you discover biblical truth for your own life and help you meet the needs of others. May God richly bless you.

For a free catalog of resources from Regal Books/Gospel Light, please call your Christian supplier or contact us at 1-800-4-GOSPEL or www.regalbooks.com.

Cover and Interior Design by Robert Williams
Edited by Joann Webster and Deena Davis

Library of Congress Cataloging-in-Publication Data
Stringer, Doug.
    Somebody Cares/Doug Stringer.
        p. cm.
    ISBN 0-8307-2860-0
    1. Somebody Cares (Organization) 2. Evangelistic work. I. Title.

BV3752.S65 S77 2001
267'.13—dc 21   2001031737

1 2 3 4 5 6 7 8 9 10 11 12 13 14 15 / 09 08 07 06 05 04 03 02 01

Rights for publishing this book in other languages are contracted by Gospel Literature International (GLINT). GLINT also provides technical help for the adaptation, translation and publishing of Bible study resources and books in scores of languages worldwide. For further information, contact GLINT, P.O. Box 4060, Ontario, CA 91761-1003, U.S.A. You may also send e-mail to Glintint@aol.com, or visit their website at www.glint.org.

I dedicate this book to my heroes of the faith. With a passion for God and a compassion for souls, you are true witnesses who rescue lives. Over the past 20 years, you have taken the DNA of this ministry from the streets of Houston, Texas, to the four corners of the world.

I am so grateful for my staff, who stand with me in the vision. You are the TEAM the Lord has raised up in this hour. To my spiritual family, it is an honor to serve you as you serve Christ.

In loving memory of those who have gone to be with the Lord: John, Mark, Bill, Brandy, Isaiah and Johnny. They overcame physical death by AIDS to gain eternity with Christ.

To all of you unknown soldiers who are sowing your lives for the gospel. May the Lord of the Harvest grant your heart's cry for spiritual awakening across the land. Together may we see with our eyes what our hearts have longed for—souls saved, lives changed and revival. As the prophet Eli spoke to Hannah, "Go in peace, and the God of Israel grant your petition which you have asked of Him" (1 Sam. 1:17).

CONTENTS

ACKNOWLEDGMENTS

Special thanks to Jack Hayford for your friendship and for introducing me to Bill Greig III and the Regal Books team.

I am so grateful to the staff of Regal Books who believe in the heartbeat of Somebody Cares. Thank you for your confidence in the message and for providing the opportunity to share it.

Thank you, Jim Buchan, for your contributions in editing. You took the manuscript to the next level. Thanks so much for being a part of the team.

Joann Webster, I want to extend my gratitude for your heart of compassion that came through as you edited this manuscript. You poured yourself into this project during a difficult season in your life. Your mother's legacy is exemplified through you.

Susie Wolf, thanks for your dedication and commitment to see the message get into people's hearts and hands.

It was the midpoint in a two-session pastors' gathering in Houston. I was the speaker and had just concluded my cup-of-tea standard for the "coffee break" in such a setting. When the emcee reassembled the more than 300 pastors who were present, I thought he was about to call me back when, instead, he asked a clear-eyed young man with a pleasant demeanor to make an announcement.

As it turned out, the announcement was about 15 minutes long—but no one in the room disapproved, and neither did I. First, because they knew—everyone in the room knew—that what was being shared was more than simply "Hey, here's what's comin' up (if you happen to care)." The announcement was detailed and the interest level was high because virtually everyone there was connected to what the young leader was talking about.

That's when I first met Doug Stringer.

It was a discovery of the first magnitude. As I listened, I turned to my host and whispered, "Who is this guy? He's got it!" Here's just a smattering of what I learned.

Doug Stringer is the driving dynamic behind *Somebody Cares, Houston*. Under the touch of the Spirit of God, he has moved into an arena of divinely given influence to unite hundreds of congregations in that city and bring about immensely wonderful and awesomely powerful things . . . as God views "powerful."

Doug Stringer is also a servant, surrendered to the spirit of sacrificial self-giving in order to answer God's call. With no guaranteed salary, he not only sold his own possessions to launch into the citywide cause he seeks to serve, but he also requires no guarantee of income to continue. Crisp and sharp in his appearance, sensitive and fluent in his communication, the last thing you would expect is a person ready to answer something like an ancient oath of poverty for the sake of ministry. Of course, that isn't exactly what Doug has done, but the spirit of such abandonment to faith for the sake of greater fruitfulness is at the root of his commitment.

Not only is Doug Stringer a voice for unity, but he also issues a clarion call that the "giants in the land" of today's cities can be conquered for the glory of God. I was moved by the visible evidence of even sometimes-cynical pastors cooperating together because of this young man who is so stirred by God and so servant-hearted in his approach to leadership.

Doug Stringer is what I call a "city saint." By that I mean he is a person like Abraham, who will intercede for a city's rescue from deserved judgment (Sodom); like Jeremiah, who will weep for a city's need and seek to call people to God's way in answering it (Jerusalem); or like Joshua, who will see the obstacle blocking a city's future and mobilize people to unite and march together until God's power changes it (Jericho).

There is a call today for city saints—for people of God who will capture a sense of His heart for their city and *live it out.*

City saints aren't spiritual gurus or people accomplished at religious exercises. They are simply willing vessels whose hearts are captivated by two things: the cry of their city's need and the possibilities of God's people making a difference.

City saints see beyond the problems and the pain of their urban environment and see the hand of God reaching out with promise *if* His people will join hands with that promise found in Jeremiah 29:7:

Seek the peace of the city where I have caused you to [come], and pray to the LORD for it; for in its peace you will have peace.

All of us live someplace where there is a cry for people who will love the needy and band together to serve them. Doug Stringer has something to say about how that can happen—anywhere, with anyone, in any church or in any town. He is a proven city saint who doesn't think anything more of himself than that he's simply your brother in Christ.

That's the best kind.

Take a couple hours and discover more of what I suddenly found in those few moments at the pastors' gathering. It will make your day and might even result in remaking your city.

Jack W. Hayford, founding pastor/president
The Church on the Way
The King's Seminary
Van Nuys, California

A story has been told that is a good illustration of where we, the Church, often find ourselves today. It is the story of fishermen who lost sight of actually catching fish.

The Parable of the Fishless Fishermen

There was once a group called the Fishermen's Fellowship. They were surrounded by streams and lakes full of hungry fish and met regularly to discuss the call to fish, the abundance of fish and the thrill of catching fish. The more they talked, the more excited they got about fishing.

Someone suggested they needed a philosophy of fishing, so they carefully defined and redefined the art and purpose of fishing. They developed elaborate fishing strategies and tactics and felt a smug satisfaction in the progress they were making toward their calling as fishermen.

One day they realized they had been going about it backwards. They had approached fishing from the point of view of the fisherman and not from the point of view of the fish. How do fish view the world? How do fishermen appear to fish? What do fish eat and when? They agreed that these are all good things to know, so they devoted themselves to researching the habits of fish and attended numerous helpful conferences on fishing. Some traveled to faraway places to study the characteristics of different kinds of fish, and one even got a Ph.D. in fishology. But no one had yet gone fishing.

So a committee was formed to send out fishermen. Since the prospective fishing places outnumbered the available fishermen, the committee needed to determine priorities. A priority list of fishing places was posted on bulletin boards in all of the group's fellowship halls. But still no one was fishing. A survey was launched to find out why. Most did not answer the survey, but from those who did, it was discovered that some felt called to study fish, a few to furnish fishing equipment and several to go around encouraging the fishermen. However, with all their meetings, conferences and committees, they simply didn't have time to fish.

Now Jake was a newcomer to the Fishermen's Fellowship. After one particularly stirring meeting of the Fellowship, Jake decided actually to go fishing. He tried some of the techniques he had heard about, got the hang of it and caught a choice fish.

At the next meeting, Jake told his story and the other fishermen were thrilled by his success. They honored him for his catch and enthusiastically scheduled him to speak at all the other Fellowship chapters and tell how he did it. Because of all the speaking invitations and his election to the board of directors of the Fishermen's Fellowship, Jake no longer had time to go fishing.

Soon, however, Jake began to feel restless and unfulfilled. He longed to feel the tug on the line once again. So he cut his busy speaking schedule, resigned from the board and said to a friend, "Let's go fishing!" They did, just the two of them, and they caught fish. The members of the Fishermen's Fellowship were many and the fish were plentiful, but the fishers were few!

PART OF THE NET

If you want a degree in fishology, don't read this book. But if you want to go out and fish, this book is for you. And take a partner—there is too much work to be done to fish with only one pole.

When Jesus first called the disciples, He called them to be fishers of men. Jesus told them to cast their net on the other side of the boat. As soon as they obeyed, they caught so many fish the net was about to break. They signaled to their partners in the other boat to come help them (see Luke 5:1-11). It is the same for us; we need each other. In fact, we cannot do this great work alone.

After Jesus' death and resurrection, Peter went back to what he knew to do—catching fish (see John 21). Jesus appeared to him at the Sea of Galilee and again instructed him and the other disciples with him to cast the net on the other side of the boat. They made a phenomenally large catch, yet their net did not break.

When we work together as the Body of Christ, we can have that same testimony. Each of us represents just one part of the net. Only by working together can we fulfill Christ's Great Commission to make disciples of all nations (see Matt. 28:19,20). The harvest will not come to its fullest extent without sacrifice and a servant's heart that says, "Whatever it takes, Lord. We will work together and get the job done."

It's all about souls—not about theories, competition or doctrinal precision. It's about bringing lost people to Christ. It's about frontline participation in the harvest. This book is a true account of what God is doing to reach the lost through people working together. We have studied the principles of evangelism long enough—it's time to put them into action.

What will it take to reach our cities? Multitudes upon multitudes are in the valley of decision between heaven and hell, and we have only a small window of time to reach them. Let's obey the Lord's command by fulfilling the Great Commission. He calls us to unite for such a time as this to fulfill our purpose and meet our date with destiny. I pray that your heart is encouraged as you read this book and that you find your place as part of a net prepared to bring in a great harvest for God's kingdom.

———————————————————————————

A true witness delivers souls, but a deceitful witness speaks lies.
PROVERBS 14:25

A TRUE WITNESS RESCUES LIVES

"You're all hypocrites!" the voice snarled. My radio host was taken aback, but I knew the caller's voice. He continued, "You bigots want to condemn everyone else to hell just because we don't do what you want."

"Mike," I said with a smile in my voice, "is that you?"

My astonished radio host looked at me with a question in his eyes that seemed to ask if he should flip the switch to cut off the caller. His call-in show drew Christian listeners, not the type he now heard. I looked at him across the microphones and smiled to allay his fears.

"What? Well . . ." the voice sputtered. This was unlike Mike, a man who had heckled at our meetings, harassed our street evangelists and hurled legal and physical threats for over a year.

"Mike, I know it's you," I said; I then addressed the listeners and my host. "This is the former president of a militant homosexual group here in Houston."

"Yeah, it's me," the voice said. "What are you going to do, get all your homophobe friends to pray for me?" His scornful laugh was weak.

"Let me ask you something, Mike." I shifted in my seat and put my face close to the microphone. "Your group hangs together, supports each other . . . all of you pretty much take each other's side, don't you?"

"Yeah!" he said, warming to the subject. "We're united, and we're gonna keep fighting until we shut you Christians up and expose you for the religious bigots you really are."

"Mike has AIDS," I told the listeners. "He's had some difficult times financially. But, Mike, you trust your friends, don't you?"

"Absolutely. They come through for me."

"Then who paid your electric bill last month?"

"What? How do you know about my electric bill?"

"Because we paid it for you, Mike."

Astonished, Mike didn't know what else to say.

Regardless of how he felt about us or what he had done to us, by coordinating with various groups in Houston, Christians were there when this AIDS patient needed help. We knew the pattern. AIDS patients' finances dwindle as they seek treatment, then their bodies betray them with loss of energy and dysfunctional organs until they can no longer care for themselves and have to depend entirely on others.

We had been believing for opportunities to reach Mike. Bill, who was also HIV-positive, had come to the Lord and was part of our ministry. Bill and others continued to reach out to Mike, and at some point, Bill went to Mike's bedside and led him to Christ. Mike cried as he received forgiveness for his sins. Within hours he left this earth and found himself in the arms of a loving Savior whom he had hated but who loved him in his sin. Another life rescued from hell's insatiable appetite.

THE BIRTH OF SOMEBODY CARES

The day I learned of Mike's salvation seemed like an eternity after my own conversion, yet it had been only 10 years. I had been a fitness instructor back then, running my own exercise studio. I knew there was a God, yet I was living as if He didn't exist. Tired of my own hypocrisy and disgusted with my life, one night I sat down in the back room of the studio, put my head in my hands and prayed a simple prayer: "Lord, if You can use someone like me after all I have done to wound Your heart, I make myself available to You."

The year was 1981. God took me at my word. It seemed the Lord couldn't find enough needy people to send my way. I ran the exercise studio and then took a group to the streets most nights after the studio closed. There we encountered the runaways, the topless dancers and the drug addicts and brought them back to the studio or to the home of a widow who had offered to help, and to Greg's apartment, which a couple of us shared with him as roommates.

We couldn't meet every need, but we were willing to do what we could. Some new converts helped me transform the exercise studio into an outreach center. By 1983, we renamed it Turning Point Studio—a Christian Activities and Fellowship Center. The turning point in my life resulted in a turning point in the lives of others who needed Christ. We called ourselves Turning Pointers.

People's needs were far greater and more complex than what our tiny band of new converts could handle, so I began linking with other ministries in Houston, and together we distributed the ordinary business card with which we Turning Pointers had started. The card simply read: "Somebody Cares at Turning Point Ministries. Call 24 hours a day. 'A true witness rescues lives . . .' Prov. 14:25." A telephone number completed the message.

I will never forget one teenager who called the telephone number saying he needed immediate help to get off the streets while he had the courage to leave. The dilemma was that my apartment was crammed with people. I gave him the telephone numbers for other ministries. He called back later with desperation in his voice, saying none would take him. I put him on hold and went to the only vacant room in the apartment. Sitting on the lid of the closed toilet, I called out to God, asking Him what to do because I couldn't turn this young man away. The Lord spoke to my heart, saying, "There's always room for one more."

I went back to the telephone and promised that we'd find a place for him, even if it were the bathtub. A volunteer picked up the young man and brought him to the apartment. Just before they arrived, the telephone rang again, this time with a ministry that had just had a vacancy. They wanted to know if I had need for another bed.

Some situations were messier. One time a bodyguard for a Dallas drug dealer called to say he was with a topless dancer and the dancer's outlaw biker husband was out to kill him because he thought they were having an affair.

I went straight to the point. "Are you having an affair?"

"Well . . . ," he stammered, before admitting it. I recommended some ministers in Dallas, but he insisted that he'd tried everyone and they all said to call me. That puzzled me. I was young and halfway in the ministry but still halfway in the business world. I had no money, no resources, no way to help anyone with anything. All I had was availability.

Although it was a financial stretch, I bought two airline tickets for the drug bodyguard and the topless dancer. The widow who had volunteered her home housed one of them and I housed the other. Shortly thereafter, both committed their lives to Christ.

Then the topless dancer's husband tracked me down and called me, screaming at me in rage. I called him a wimp and said if he were a real man he would submit himself to Christ and learn how to love his wife. Right there, during the telephone call, he started crying and said he was coming down to Houston, too. He came, got saved, stayed for quite a while to be discipled, got back together with his wife; and the two of them left. The bodyguard also eventually left and is on staff with a Christian drug rehab center today.

From such simple beginnings, the "Somebody Cares" message spread. We were a bunch of young people without money or official church support, yet we provided temporary housing for the homeless, conducted street witnessing and evangelistic crusades, did Jericho Marches around rock concerts and sponsored other activities geared to fellowship and discipleship. Drug addicts, alcoholics, homosexuals, topless dancers and prostitutes—people considered too far gone by many—came to know Christ and are now in good churches, jobs, businesses and ministries.

All those years ago, when God grabbed hold of my heart, I knew if He could save me, He could save others. God established the heart of the ministry then and it has never changed, even though it has expanded to include not only meeting the needs of individuals but has also allowed us to network and share the vision with other cities and with nations about how believers can make a difference in their world.

Internationally we are networking and linking with ministries, churches, schools, governments and community leaders worldwide with the same message carried by the original little business card: "A true witness rescues lives" (or saves souls). We are not just an outreach of one group or denomination. Rather, we represent a united outreach of individual communities that includes feeding centers, crisis pregnancy intervention, AIDS relief, gang prevention, men's and women's homes, drug abuse recovery, borderline teen intervention, foster care, job placement and more. It is a joy to see what God has done in and through us as we join together to win our cities to Christ.

THE URGENCY OF THE HOUR

The message inherent in the words "Somebody Cares" is one that all people everywhere long to hear. Take for example a trip I made to Indonesia in 1998. Ministers in Indonesia had requested that I speak at a large prayer conference. A dear friend, Paul Tan, had started the Indonesian Relief Fund, on whose advisory board I serve. I responded to the pastors' request with a request of my own. If I came to minister at their conference, I wanted them to set up feeding centers where Christians would provide food for the poor during the days I was there.

I made this request at a time of political turmoil. Militants were hunting and slaughtering Christians in some parts of the nation. Many Christians had lost their jobs and businesses, and many had fled the country. Headlines worldwide trumpeted the failed economy and national crisis in this fourth-largest nation on Earth, home to the world's largest Muslim population.

The Indonesian ministers said they had nothing to give, so I asked them just to do what Jesus did when He faced a hungry multitude and had only a child's lunch with which to feed them. Take what you have, bless it, and start giving it away. They agreed to try.

As a result of the Christians' efforts to feed the poor, one hundred pastors were asked to meet with then President Habibi, and they invited me to come to the meeting. I hated to change my airline ticket because I didn't have the money for the additional expense; but the ministers urged me that this was unprecedented in their nation's history. I agreed to join them. During the meeting, President Habibi, on national television, praised the efforts and compassion of these Christians and officially endorsed what became known as Somebody Cares Indonesian Movement.

A team from Houston, comprised of Hispanics, Asians, pastors and intercessors, accompanied me to Indonesia. Once there, we saw what the impoverished Christians had accomplished. Pastor Jimmy and his group had set up 35 feeding centers called Free Lunch from the Lord, Somebody Cares.

After ministering at their conference, they took our team to outlying areas so we could minister to the rural poor. We drove in vans from location to location. Pastors grimaced as they saw settlements of hundreds of people living in garbage dumps and hundreds more under bridges. A few of the pastors had never traveled outside their area to see the plight of their people. At one stop in a mountain village, a local pastor introduced us to a young man.

"He has won his entire village to Christ," the pastor announced through interpreters.

"Then I need to wash his feet," I said, "because I have not yet won mine."

Some of the pastors seemed dismayed at my request but they found a bowl of water and some rags. I was sincere in honoring this young man for winning his city.

Afterwards, the pastors loaded back into the vans and traveled to the next stop in silence as the impact of what they had just witnessed settled over them. When I asked about their silence, they said they were speechless because an American minister had washed the feet of one of their poorest countrymen. When we returned to Jakarta, one pastor told the others, "This man didn't honor us for holding a nationwide event, but he honored the man who had led every person he knew to Christ. He has shown us what truly matters."

Traveling on to Malaysia, the movement we left behind spread and gained momentum. I received a call at my hotel room and learned that the governor of Java now wanted to meet with me and help us bring to his area the Somebody Cares Indonesia feeding centers, as they were now being called. Again, I changed my airline tickets and went back to accompany local pastors to the governor's mansion. God gave me a prophetic message for this Muslim leader: If he blessed God's people, God would bless him. He bowed his head and said he wanted to be a friend. He, too, went on television to endorse the Somebody Cares movement.

THE CREATOR OF THE UNIVERSE INTENDS FOR YOUR LIFE AND MINE TO SHAPE THE DESTINY OF THIS WORLD.

During the eight months after we left, Indonesian Christians managed to feed 3 million people. The pastors were overjoyed that as the Christians gave, God multiplied their efforts until sites in several cities provided "Lunch from the Lord," based on what Jesus had done with the hungry multitude. They followed the Somebody Cares model and involved hundreds of churches and ministries to accomplish their agenda. When they came together in unity, even a seemingly hostile government had to acknowledge them.

With just a glance at world crises such as Indonesia's, it is impossible to ignore the intensity and urgency of the hour. Simply by being born to this generation, you and I have been called for such a time as this to reach out to people—from pau-pers to presidents.

The Creator of the universe intends for your life and mine to shape the destiny of this world. When I met Christ, some-thing changed inside me so that I no longer lived just for myself. My life was not my own. The day any of us comes to Christ, our lives have new meaning and purpose. Our Father has a job for us to accomplish.

Jesus revealed Himself that we might have a relationship with Him, but that's not all. As an outcome of that relationship, we are called to be ministers of reconciliation and witnesses who rescue lives (see Acts 26:16; Prov. 14:25). We can impact this generation with the gospel of Christ, which is the power of God for salvation to all who believe (see Rom. 1:16).

We have a window of time to reach the multitudes still in the valley of decision. The question is, Will we answer the call? To say yes, we must understand the awesome responsibility God has entrusted to us, His Church.

MINISTERS OF RECONCILIATION

In 1983, I was driving with a 16-year-old street kid who hadn't eaten in four days and was looking for a ministry which could care for him. On the way back to Houston on Highway 59, I saw a hitchhiker with a sign that said "Australian." As I passed the hitchhiker, God spoke to my heart to stop, so I pulled over, backed up and picked him up. That one act unwittingly started him on the ride of his life.

"G'day mate," Andrew Merry said as he jumped into the car. He asked if I would drive him to a youth hostel to stay for a night. He explained that he was traveling casually on a one-year trip to see the world. I told him he could ride with us to my exercise studio and I'd try to find a place for him to stay. I left Andrew and the street kid to sleep in one room while I went to my office to make some calls. After a while, Andrew came in, asking about the street kid. The teenager had run off with Andrew's backpack, which among other things held his passport and money.

As a result, Andrew was stuck in Houston much longer than he had planned. Before landing in Houston, Andrew had met a young New Zealand woman named Lynette, who was also traveling around the world on a one-year pass. Lynette had just become a Christian before leaving for overseas and realized she would be better off without a non-Christian boyfriend. She resisted Andrew's romantic interest and they remained friends.

On Andrew's second or third night in Houston, I took him to a Christian concert at Astroworld. He was amazed at what Christianity actually meant. Within a few days, he gave his heart to Christ and decided to stay with us for six weeks to become discipled and grounded in his new faith. I have never seen a young convert soak in the gospel as quickly and earnestly as Andrew Merry did.

He regaled us with stories of his life Down Under. Andrew was a triathlete and a coach who had tried hard to party his life away. While driving drunk just before leaving the country, he heard something say, "Slow down." He immediately slowed his car. Rounding the next corner, he saw a person who had fallen in the street and whom he would have run over had he not slowed the car. Clearly God was directing Andrew's steps.

Finally the day came for us to bid Andrew farewell so he could continue on to Europe, via New York, where he met up with Lynette again. Naturally, he couldn't wait to tell Lynette he was now a Christian, but she ignored him, believing he was just trying to impress her. Andrew's new habit of witnessing to others eventually won her over. While in Europe, their friendship

began to blossom. By the time they returned to their own countries, Andrew had changed so much that his testimony was writ-
ten up in the local newspapers. Andrew and Lynette continued
their correspondence and later became engaged.

Today they have three beautiful children and pastor a thriving church, Ocean Grove Baptist Fellowship. Andrew is also
involved in a branch of a national Australian Bible college. They
continue to relate to and connect with Turning Point Ministries
International and are implementing the Somebody Cares concept in their area.

On the road to Damascus, Jesus said to Saul, "I have appeared
to you for this purpose, to make you a minister and a witness"
(Acts 26:16). Jesus revealed Himself first for the sake of saving
Saul, but also so that Saul would fulfill a God-ordained purpose.
This was what Andrew also learned.

The first revelation any of us receive from God is the revelation of the work of the Cross—that we have been bought with
Christ's own blood shed on Calvary—and the power of His resurrection. This is the revelation of Jesus, our Savior and our
Redeemer, that leads us to salvation. In that redemption we are
given a greater purpose.

When he received his commission from the Lord, Saul
became an apostle of the good news. God changed his name to
Paul to sever ties with his old identity and old life. Paul now
burned with a holy passion to make Christ known. He was a catalyst for whole villages and cities coming to Christ. He wrote:

> Much more then, having now been justified by His
> blood, we shall be saved from wrath through Him. For if
> when we were enemies we were reconciled to God
> through the death of His Son, much more, having been
> reconciled, we shall be saved by His life. And not only
> that, but we also rejoice in God through our Lord Jesus

Christ, through whom *we have now received the reconciliation* (Rom. 5:9-11, emphasis mine).

Through the blood of God's Son we are reconciled to Him and made joint heirs with Christ. "[We give] thanks to the Father who has qualified us to be partakers of the inheritance of the saints in the light" (Col. 1:12). Once we were separated from the Father by our sin, but now we are redeemed and restored to a right relationship with Him. No greater peace or joy exists than to know we belong to Christ. But this is just the beginning of our journey as believers.

Therefore, if anyone is in Christ, he is a new creation; old things have passed away; behold, all things have become new. Now all things are of God, who has reconciled us to Himself through Jesus Christ, and has given us the ministry of reconciliation, that is, that God was in Christ reconciling the world to Himself, not imputing their trespasses to them, and *has committed to us the word of reconciliation.*

Now then, we are ambassadors for Christ, as though God were pleading through us: we implore you on Christ's behalf, be reconciled to God. For He made Him who knew no sin to be sin for us, that we might become the righteousness of God in Him (2 Cor. 5:17-21, emphasis mine).

As soon as we are reconciled to Christ, we become *ministers* of reconciliation. That is our calling. Regardless of the specific way in which we serve God's kingdom, our primary purpose is to minister to others.

As we live purposefully before the Lord, our lives exude the Lord's presence, and others are drawn to Him through us to find their place of reconciliation with the living God. People all around us are searching and longing for the hope they see living inside of you and me. How will they know this hope unless we are faithful to be His witnesses?

Before Andrew exercised his gifts or talents, he first became a minister of reconciliation right where he was to those around him. Hundreds have now come to Christ through his ministry of reconciliation, which is his first and basic purpose.

Passion for God and the Lost

A passion for God compels us to share the good news with the lost. Yet how many of us have questioned if God can truly use us to reach the lost? Many believers wonder what they have to offer, not realizing the power of God's Spirit abiding in them. The same power that resurrected Christ from the dead dwells in our mortal bodies (see Rom. 8:11). God does not entrust us with this power so that we can glory in it. His power dwells in us so His love can flow through us, drawing others to Him.

We are never too insignificant, too unnoticed or too weak to exercise God's power. Some people point to a Scripture about judgments of the last days, with earthquakes and famines (see Luke 21:11). But even though God says a shaking is coming (see Heb. 12:26), one sentence pops out: "it will turn out for you as an occasion for testimony" (Luke 21:13). Bad news, weakness and difficulty are opportunities for the Christian.

No matter what you and I may go through, regardless of the circumstances of our lives or the setbacks we face, we have the opportunity for our lives to be a witness to others. Whatever the trials, we will overcome by the blood of the Lamb and the word of our testimony (see Rev. 12:11). We will see all things work together for the good of those who love God and are called according to His purpose (see Rom. 8:28). No matter the intensity, there will be an opportunity for our witness and our testimony. The question is, Will we recognize the opportunity?

Almost two years after Mike, the radio caller, died from AIDS, I was ministering at a local church in another city in Texas, where I told Mike's story. After the meeting, a woman came to me, crying. The harder she tried to speak, the more she seemed to cry.

"That," she blurted out at last, "was my son."

For years she had prayed for Mike, even though their relationship was strained because of his lifestyle and activism against everything that had to do with her God. Yet while he lived, she had prayed. She did her part. Others did their parts. As a result, today Mike is in heaven with our Lord.

We live in awesome times. Let's not miss our opportunities. The job at hand is larger than any one person, church or ministry can handle. We can only reach our communities if we all work together. It starts by each of us individually asking the Lord how we are to exercise our ministry of reconciliation and how we are to link up with others in the Body of Christ.

*But rise and stand on your feet; for I have appeared to you for this purpose, to
make you a minister and a witness both of the things which you have seen and
of the things which I will yet reveal to you.*

A C T S   2 6 : 1 6

SOMETHING
BIGGER THAN
OURSELVES

One night in the early '80s, a young couple stood on a street corner
in the Montrose area of Houston, which at that time had one of the
highest crime rates in Texas. Montrose, also called Lower
Westheimer, was a haven for runaways and filled with prostitutes,
drug dealers, homosexuals and pimps. Making it even worse, even
youth and yuppies from suburbia found their entertainment cruising Lower Westheimer on weekend nights. Their presence and economic support helped establish a sad and perverse lifestyle.

The young couple on the corner looked typical—young
teenagers who had no means of support other than to sell them-

selves on the streets. It was apparent they had lived on the streets for a while, even though their youthfulness had not yet given way to hardness. Lori was cute, with delicate features and a soft voice. In any home in America her mother would have scolded her for wearing too much makeup. She was attractive enough without it. Brandon was thin, still not filled out, with sad eyes and dirty-blond hair. He smelled of cigarettes and sweat.

What captured my heart was the stroller between them. Children with children of their own. The stroller held a precious newborn and a toddler and was parked right in front of a pay phone where Lori and Brandon took their calls. They would wait for the phone to ring, then Brandon would watch the children while Lori waded through the bumper-to-bumper traffic to find the caller and turn a trick. If the call was for Brandon, Lori would baby-sit while Brandon serviced the caller.

Such a sight still overwhelms me. When I see it I want to run up and yell, "Stop! You don't have to live like this. Quick, come with me!" That's about what I did with Brandon and Lori. I told them the good news of the gospel and shared with them my care and concern, convincing them to come home with me.

After I had been in this ministry for a while, E. Z. Jones, who led a local men's ministry, paid for me to have my own apartment. At one point, 17 people lived in it with me. I didn't have the funds to feed anyone, but I took Brandon and Lori and their children home anyway, believing that a night in my home even without food would be better than a night on the streets.

One day E. Z. came to the apartment and saw all the people. He gave me one of those blank, disbelieving looks and said, "Doug, how are you feeding all these people?"

I smiled and told him we trusted the Lord to provide each day.

We had witnessed true miracles of God's provision as we prayed and stayed focused on our calling. People would leave groceries at the door or provide for our needs in other ways. God does not ask the same of every person, but He does ask each of us to do what we can. We proved that even a home-cooked meal could be a part of fulfilling God's call.

E. Z.'s heart was touched by what he saw. He and his wife, Lena, started providing food for inner-city ministries by establishing a Christian businessmen's network known as Luv Ya Houston. E. Z. recognized what we were learning—that each of us has a vital role in reaching people within our communities.

Through those early experiences in reaching out to people like Brandon and Lori, I saw a glimpse of what God intended for every believer. The job was far bigger than anyone could handle alone. The number of homeless people, drug addicts and troubled teens is enormous. Other lost people cover their true needs with masks of success and affluence. Whatever the situation, every person is hungry for truth and for love. And all believers are called to become *part of something bigger than themselves* to extend that love .

When all believers—the Body of Christ—work together, we can meet people's physical needs. People who encounter our true care and concern for them are drawn to the love of Christ operating in us. Each individual, each church or ministry, working together and doing its part, can impact a whole city with the gospel.

In the case of Lori and Brandon, the call of the streets was stronger than their ability to resist. Time and again they returned to their dangerous lifestyle. They eventually contracted diseases and lost their children to state government. Their young, promising lives are coming to an end without ever fulfilling their potential. Yet they know who Jesus is.

We may work with an individual off and on for many years before the breakthrough comes in his or her life. Sometimes we never see it. Yet no labor for the Lord is in vain. God is faithful to watch over every seed sown into a soul.

WE ARE THE ONLY PLAN GOD HAS

Pastor Bill Anderson of Calvary Baptist Church, who is part of Somebody Cares Tampa Bay, shared this story from his childhood at one of their meetings in 1997:

> God stabbed my heart about unity long before I was saved. My father was killed in an oil field accident when I was just five weeks old. My dear mother, who lives in Clearwater, Florida, now is 98 years old and loves God with all her heart. One day as young teenagers, my sister and I were fighting. My mother came to me and it was one of the rare times that I saw fear in her eyes. She is a very strong woman. She had to be, for more than 60 years now she has been without a man by her side. Raising four children by herself, she made it one day at a time, as she says, "by the grace of God."
>
> Mother sat my sister and me down and wept as she said, "You *have* to get along, because you're all I have." That stabbed me.
>
> Listen, there are not two brides. There's only one Bride. We are the only Bride Christ has. If we don't do it right, nobody can.

God has no other plan. We are it. That means He has confidence that Christ in us can meet the challenge. Our common purpose is to see lost souls come to the Lord. Jesus showed us that a grain of seed must die for there to be fruitfulness (see John 12:24). This is true in our lives individually, as we die to our own agendas, and it is true for the Body of Christ.

We are called to sow the seed of our lives into the soil of souls. This doesn't mean we come together in unity only for citywide Christian gatherings but that we desire to see lives changed—

people turned from darkness to light (see Acts 26:18). We're not looking for unity for unity's sake, because unity never works without a purpose. And that's the point of Acts 26. Unity is not the goal; it is the by-product.

LET US LOOK FOR UNITY WITH THE HIGHEST COMMON DENOMINATOR— A PASSION FOR GOD AND COMPASSION FOR SOULS.

To have genuine unity, we have to have a purpose far greater than ourselves. Let us not look for unity as the lowest common denominator, which always leads to compromise. Let us look for unity with the highest common denominator—a great purpose found in passion for God and compassion for souls.

We are called to reach the unchurched with the good news, which we've traditionally called revival. If what we do doesn't equate into changed lives and lost souls coming to Christ, it falls short of being a true revival.

THEY SAID IT WOULDN'T LAST

From our beginnings in the early 1980s, our Turning Point Ministries group made ongoing efforts to network ministries and churches. By the mid-1980s we were serving alongside other ministries on a regular basis. Relationships blossomed and strengthened as we all worked together in weekly street evangelism. Unknown soldiers of the gospel reached out to prostitutes, drug addicts and street kids for years. They are true heroes of God's kingdom.

Starting in 1986, and for 10 years afterward, Turning Point Ministries sponsored an annual evangelism conference to link inner-city ministries with mainline suburban churches. We provided a place to share strategies and establish a system of referral to help those in need.

People told me that a conference focusing on unifying the Body of Christ toward a common goal seemed far-fetched and wouldn't work. Critics said churches and other ministries would not work together because they wanted to do their own thing. So I prayed about it and got together with other local ministers. We decided that regardless of who might not cooperate, many would, and it was time to combine forces! We set these goals:

Synergy. We recognized that unifying various ministries would enlarge and augment the efforts of each ministry working on its own and promote fruitfulness.

Referrals. We committed to establishing a referral list of proven ministries.

Guidance. We endeavored to give guidance to people who wanted to serve God but didn't know how.

Honoring the local church. We encouraged people to support, encourage and work in their local churches.

The bottom line was and is to serve the people who need ministry. Too many times we don't know what to do with people who have AIDS, who are runaways or are church members whose children are involved in gangs. Certainly every church and ministry can't operate its own hospice, feeding center or home for unwed mothers. But linked together these same churches and ministries can say, "Wait a minute, I know who can help you!"

The annual conference allowed us to recognize ministries already functioning in our city and, in some cases, it birthed new ministries. As we combined the outreach efforts into one place we discovered areas of need the Church had not yet addressed. For example, God touched people's hearts to work with the Houston police department when we realized there were no Christians active in dealing with the gang problem.

At one conference, John Hazzard brought the audience to tears. He was the least likely person anyone would have expected to get saved. A drug mule for nationally organized gangs, he was AIDS-infected from sharing needles while shooting heroin, a habit acquired at age 14. Members of our ministry team worked with John when he became serious about God, and he became a changed man.

John had been in several drug rehabilitation centers and mental hospitals and only had a third-grade education. We found a tutor to help him learn to read and write, so he could study the Bible for himself. His first volunteer project at our office was to put our rolodex in alphabetical order.

When John was told he had only six months to live, a tutor might have seemed an extravagance, but John lived for another four years and became an integral part of the ministry.

We made a multipurpose room filled with boxes and equipment available to John and anyone else who wandered in. In it we placed a donated television, VCR and stacks of Christian teaching tapes like those found in the homes of many Christians. Those tapes discipled John while we were busy. One-on-one discipleship occurred in the evenings. Soon John began volunteering to help with mailings and then to reach out to others.

Through John and his ministry, God opened doors for the salvation of many others who needed freedom from various bondages and addictions. Five prayer and discipleship groups sprang up. Close friendships developed between John and several people, including Gabi Soltau, a missionary from Germany, who joined the Turning Point team. She now travels abroad, reproducing the DNA of this ministry as she teaches on prayer.

When I took John with me to Houston Baptist University to help teach a friend's class, the distinguished Bible instructor came to John afterward, shook his hand, and said he'd never heard anyone lay out Scripture as John had.

As John's body deteriorated from AIDS, his light shone brighter and brighter. He opened his home to some and continued to witness with us. He went on 14 missionary trips, even as his body wasted away.

His T cell count was only 23 and he weighed just 80 pounds when he asked one of our ministers to take him to buy five new shirts, which he washed and ironed himself to attend what would be his last conference. At the conference, he encouraged each of us to do what God says, to set aside differences and combine our efforts to reach others like him who only needed an opportunity to hear the truth. He battled for every breath, and each word gripped our hearts.

At that conference, John shared one of his favorite quotes by Andrew Murray (1828-1917), a preacher in Scotland and South Africa: "Give up on no man as long as he is alive; until he is laid in the grave, give up on no man." After John said this, he looked at a few of us and said, "I thank God that Doug and George and all of my Turning Point family did not give up on me."

Sounding a Trumpet

At each of these annual conferences we focused on a specific theme, such as "revival equates into changed lives" or "evangelism is an outcome of relationship," always stressing that we must *become part of something bigger than ourselves*. Workshops equipped Christian workers. Ministers and laypersons alike challenged participants to submit to their local churches, to work with other ministers, to exercise spiritual warfare, to stand in the gap for souls and to look beyond their immediate communities to impact the entire city.

Over a period of years we challenged participants to commit to the motto "A Call to Consecration and Action." This phrase is part of the mission statement Turning Point has used since the early '80s. The Lord is calling for a united Church, which requires a message of

Consecration: being separated unto God, recognizing His holiness, our own unrighteousness and His grace;

Commitment: not just "romancing" God and His work but acknowledging our responsibility to obey Him and letting that knowledge provoke us to action;

Action: turning our responsibility into concrete obedience.

Today, Turning Point's mission statement is "Preparing a people for the coming of the Lord through a message of *consecration, commitment* and *action*." From our individual relationships with the Lord, we commit to availability for His service. We must move beyond declarations and proclamations into action and become a tangible expression of Christ. Then we unite as the Body of Christ and take action to reach out with the gospel.

When we do these things, the Lord *will* transform our communities.

But it takes prayer, diligence and consistency to see breakthroughs. Already we are seeing communities change as the Church agrees to work together for the common purpose of reaching the lost and the unchurched.

The synergy created when ministries work together exponentially increases our potential to impact lives. One group may have a gift to work with unwed mothers, while another group provides legal services for them. Another ministry will work with those who are HIV-positive, while a partner church provides food and clothing. If a homeless shelter is in disrepair, a ministry provides the volunteers to renovate it.

IF WE WANT TRUE REVIVAL, WE MUST BE WILLING TO GET PAST DIFFERENCES WITHIN THE BODY OF CHRIST.

There is hope for our generation, and we are called to share that hope. But seeing God's kingdom built requires sacrifice and dying to our own rights and agendas. To fulfill our purpose of leading a generation to Christ, not only must we be reconciled to God, but we must also be reconciled to one another. The world is looking for answers. God will draw them to us for those answers as they see our love for Him and for each other.

Revival will not come unless we are willing to get past the things that have hindered our relationship with the Lord and with our brothers and sisters in Christ. If we want true revival, we must be willing to work with brothers and sisters of a different denomination or nationality. We must be willing to get past differences within the Body of Christ. And most important, we must be in right relationship with God and with those in the Church.

ONE CHURCH, ONE PURPOSE

Eventually more than 200 ministries and churches agreed to work together to impact the greater Houston area. Turning Point Ministries was the umbrella organization that allied them into a network known as Somebody Cares. Many ministers signed a covenant of unity, stating that because they agreed on the basic tenets of their faith, they would work together, serve one another and keep the unity of their faith and fellowship. I also call it the "no competition" clause.

These ministers were not just *talking* about the problems in their city, they were *working* in practical ways to impact the city at a grassroots level. Unity with a purpose is an action and a commitment to see a great harvest, not only in a particular city but also across this nation and in all the nations of the world.

Somebody Cares has not actually created a new work; it has merely identified what God is already doing. Ministers and their congregants, who are already touching lives, are linking arms with others who are doing the same. We recognize that we are not the only network; we simply desire to identify and link together those who are already reaching out at a grassroots level.

The heart of Somebody Cares can be summed up in the slight change of words we made to that business card from decades ago: "Somebody Cares. Because of what Jesus Christ has done for us, area churches and ministries want you to know that we care." This is a message that communicates to the unchurched that God cares for them, and He cares for them through you and me.

JOY IN THE HARVEST

What joy we experience when even one person responds to the gospel! It may take years to see the fruit of our labors, and after countless hours of witnessing and counseling there is often heartbreak when the truth is rejected. Yet each person who receives and accepts help is one more soul snatched from the devil's clutches.

Years after the day I brought Brandon and Lori into my apartment—a ministry attempt that could be viewed as a dismal failure—I met a couple, Dick and Debbie Byerley, whose mission is to adopt and rehabilitate discarded children. They heard me talk about "throwaway" children at a Turning Point conference in 1989, and the term captured their hearts. A week later they were asked to provide foster care for a child from Casa de Esperanza, a Catholic-run orphanage. The child was the hardest case the orphanage had ever handled. Then the Byerleys received the child's sibling. They eventually adopted both children.

Through a coincidence that can only have come through the faithfulness of God, their two adopted children are Brandon and Lori's precious little ones who were raised on the streets while their parents prostituted themselves. Our heavenly Father was looking out for those precious babies all along. God is a Father to the fatherless (see Ps. 68:5).

Dick and Debbie have adopted a total of seven children. When combined with the 10 children in their blended family, they have a grand total of 17 children. They have mastered the governmental red tape that scares most people away from adoption and discovered that nearly 800 throwaway children exist in the Houston area. These could easily be absorbed by a small fraction of the number of Christian families in the area.

The children the Byerleys have adopted are considered high risk and they still have their struggles. Some may stay in Dick and Debbie's care for life, but the family is working well. Two of their children came from a home where they had to fight the family pets for food. The parents thought it was amusing to set the dog and cat food on the floor and watch their child fight the animals for the right to eat. One of their children, who now enjoys a home, family, siblings, food and clothing, was interviewed early in the adoption process. She had come from living in a field, then was found abandoned in a boxcar. The interviewers asked her, "Did you have a tent in that field?" "No," she responded, "but sometimes we had newspapers."

One child couldn't sleep at night, so one of Dick and Debbie's grown children used to crawl into the crib to sleep with her. Another was so afraid of men she couldn't allow herself to get near Dick. Recently I was shown proud photos of her "first date." It was with Dick, her daddy, who had brought flowers and picked up his daughter to take her out to dinner. Simple for some, yet a milestone for this girl.

Government agencies have observed the love and care that children receive in Dick and Debbie's home. They've noticed the remarkable changes in the lives of these young people who came from such abusive backgrounds that it was feared they would be marked for life. They are marked for life—life more abundant through Jesus. They are working through their issues, not running from them or covering them up. They are finding healing and freedom, and no one would guess what they've been through. The love of Jesus has brought wholeness to their lives.

Dick and Debbie Byerley are part of a team from Somebody Cares Houston that is developing Hope in Houston, a citywide Church effort to see Houston's 800 orphans adopted. Over 100 people from a dozen churches came to hear the first presentation. The Byerleys are linking government and private agencies with the Body of Christ to place these children, and they're off to a great start.

What About Your City?

What has taken place and is continuing to take place in Houston can happen anywhere. What about your city? Do you have a strategy to work with other believers to reach your city? There's no better time to get started than now.

I thank God for the various ministries reaching out in Houston and for the results of their outreach as a network. When I pray for His Touch Ministries, a work that cares for those who are HIV-positive, I am reminded of the HIV-positive people who have come through Turning Point—John, Isaiah, Johnny, Bill, Mark and others who have now gone home to be with Jesus because of this terrible disease. Our ministry team understands the sleepless nights, the round-the-clock care required and the grief of family members. And our hearts go out to the ones ministering to those needs.

The Spanish-language Somebody Cares, called Alguien Se Interesa, is reaching the Hispanic community, which accounts for 30 percent of Houston's 4.5 million people. Due to the efforts of men such as Dr. DeLeon, Pastor Jiminez, Pastor Salazar, Pastor Sanchez, Pastor Dicesare and others, Hispanic ministries and churches are uniting to reach this large community in our city. Through cooperative efforts, Somebody Cares has distributed the Alguien Se Interesa Bible across the city.

As I pray for Victory Inner-City Ministries and their work with former drug addicts and gang members, I remember Robert, a former gang member who got out of the gang, avoided attempted hits on his life and yet died of cancer. Months before his death, Robert gave his life to Christ. I spoke with him just days before his death and asked if there was anything we could do for him. His only concern was for his wife and child. He is remembered as a loving husband and father because he became a new man in Christ.

I also remember ministering at a memorial service for a teen killed in a drive-by gang shooting. He was a junior high school student killed for his "designer" athletic shoes.

These stories are about real people who left family members behind. That is why the work of each ministry is so vital. My heart is stirred to stand in the gap for frontline workers and the people they reach. These people need encouragement to press on each day and not become weary in well-doing (see Gal. 6:9).

There are so many still to be reached! Together, with each of us doing our part, we can make a difference. If we walk in a right relationship with the Lord and with each other, His light will shine through us and draw people to Him.

How will our communities be reached? By our *intercession* and then our *intervention* for the multitudes hanging in the balance of eternity.

We were well pleased to impart to you not only the gospel of God, but also our
own lives, because you had become dear to us.

1   T H E S S A L O N I A N S   2 : 8

A KINGDOM
BUILT ON
RELATIONSHIP

Etched into my heart are the names and faces of the people we reached on the streets in those early years. Some did not make it out of street life. Some did but died young due to the consequences of their choices. There are, however, many success stories of young men and women who left street life behind. Not only were they discipled, but they also became active in discipling others. There is no greater joy than seeing a wayward life radically turned around by God.

As we worked on the streets and as the network of ministries we worked with began to grow, we realized that the kingdom of

God is built on relationship. As friendships formed between young ministers and laypersons who had the same heartbeat to reach hurting people, God began to link us together to address the diverse situations we encountered.

Not everyone is called to street ministry or to the inner cities, but each of us is called to fulfill the work of an evangelist (see 2 Tim. 4:5). Not everyone has a special gift as an evangelist, but we can all be living witnesses (see Acts 1:8; Eph. 4:11). Each day our lives can testify of Christ's love, and we can do our part as we develop our relationship with the Lord and He gives us His heart for people.

HAND IN HAND TO REACH THE LOST

"Mohawk" frequented the Lower Westheimer area of Houston where the street kids hung out. Covered with tattoos and filled with hatred, the only people he got along with were skinheads. As a person of Asian descent, I was the unlikeliest person this skinhead would listen to, let alone trust.

Still, when I saw Mohawk sitting on a curb, I would sit down to talk with him. Soon he actually wanted to spend time with me. We started working out at a gym together, and eventually I could tell that his initial hatred toward me was gone. Mohawk was building a respect toward the people of God, which translated into a respect toward the things of God. Love was beginning to break through.

As teams of ministers worked with Mohawk and others like him, this young man and the other street kids saw love in action. A local Baptist minister named Curt Williams had come to the streets independently and joined me on many nights to talk with young people. We established a place called The Refuge at 408 Westheimer, right in the middle of the kids' hangout area.

Volunteers staffed it. The young people knew that when they wanted help, regardless of the time of day or night, someone would be there for them.

When the *Houston Chronicle* ran a story about street evangelism and the change it was bringing to the city's young people, Curt and I told the reporters that our mission was not just to get troubled teens off the streets but also to get them into environments where they could quit running from their problems. When the kids said they wanted help, we either provided them housing or referred them to someone who could put them up.

Based on Curt's heart's desire to disciple young men once they left street life, he and his wife, Shelley, founded Youth-Reach Houston, which is a licensed foster home for teenage boys. I am honored to serve on Youth-Reach's board of advisors. For years now, Youth-Reach has been an outstanding ministry for discipling young people in our city. They now are working in southeast Texas and Tennessee as well.

Beyond Survival to Discipleship

Every street kid I've ever met has the need to be loved and to belong to a family. In their street culture vernacular they often say, "If one of us is in trouble, we cut for each other," meaning they stand up for each other. They're saying they're one family, one culture and have one purpose—survival—but this is true only to a point. In the game of survival, each person ultimately ends up looking out for himself.

Over time, Mohawk realized there was more to life than just survival on the streets. He eventually succumbed to regular, healthy doses of love and left street life and his street name behind. Today he helps other young people at Youth-Reach Houston and is known as a young successful Christian counselor named Dave. We praise God for the dramatic changes in Dave's life. At the same time, we recognize that many more like him still need to be reached.

At times the Lord may speak to our hearts about an entire people group for whom we are to pray and reach out to with the gospel message. But how do we minister to different nationalities and cultures? What will it take to understand them and meet their needs? Understanding begins with gaining an appreciation for those in the Body of Christ who come from different backgrounds. As we learn to love and care for each other, we will likewise be able to minister to unbelievers in various people groups.

The Body of Christ's ability to embrace different groups must begin with each believer's own desire. As each of us gets to know Christian brothers and sisters of different cultural groups and we come to understand the issues they face, we will see how much we need one another in order to make a difference in people's lives. We may not be able to reach a particular community others have been called to serve, but we can support their efforts and build each other up.

PREPARING THE BRIDE

God is preparing a Bride for His Son. Part of that preparation is the necessity of getting past obstacles that hinder our relationships within the Body of Christ.

The Bride God is preparing is radiant with His character and full of charity, with no division in her heart. She does not quarrel over rights or set boundaries for her service. She willingly offers herself for the sake of the Bridegroom.

The prophet Micah wrote about the people of God who will gather at His holy mountain to form a strong nation (see Mic. 4:1-

7). This is a theme that challenges us to lay down our weapons of warfare and exchange them with harvesting tools.

> He shall judge between many peoples, and rebuke strong nations afar off; they shall beat their swords into plow-shares, and their spears into pruning hooks; nation shall not lift up sword against nation, neither shall they learn war anymore (Mic. 4:3).

As we gather together with a passion for God and with compassion for those who do not yet know the Lord, we can become the Bride described in biblical prophecy. This kind of unity will only occur as we focus on the harvest, which is God's primary calling to the Church today. In the world we will continue to hear of warring factions, but there is a group of people who are setting aside their differences, adopting a common identity and a common purpose to overcome a common enemy.

Micah goes on to speak of the kind of people who will make up the harvest: "'In that day,' says the LORD, 'I will assemble the lame, I will gather the outcast, and those whom I have afflicted; I will make the lame a remnant, and the outcast a strong nation'" (Mic. 4:6,7). What a beautiful sight that will be! Already the Lord is beginning to gather His people in such a way, taking outcasts and making us into "a strong nation." It is not unlike the weaving of multicolored threads into a finished fabric.

A Coat of Many Colors

In Genesis 37 we read about a beautifully woven coat presented to Joseph by his father Jacob. Imagine for a moment the beauty of the tunic coat Jacob gave to Joseph. That coat must have been brilliant in color and quality. As its colors were interwoven, a beautiful fabric emerged.

When I think of the coat of many colors, I see a picture of the Bride God desires to present to Jesus Christ. As the Body of Christ becomes a united Bride, we become a coat woven together of many colors. Though we are diverse in ethnicity and culture, through Christ we are knit together from every background to become a strong nation. We are now part of the culture of Christ.

Something happened after Joseph received the coat; his brothers resented him for the favor he received from his father and for the dream he shared with them. In their jealousy they sought to destroy Joseph. A similar scenario can happen within the Body of Christ. We must guard against animosity, jealousy, envy or bitterness that would divide us from other brothers and sisters. It could be that some have a different vision, or perhaps we are jealous of the way God is blessing another's ministry. This must not happen. We must also recognize and repent of any prejudices against other nationalities.

I'm not talking about an ideal. This unity has been achieved in the Somebody Cares network. Unity, which has come about gradually, has accelerated since the mid-'90s. Let me tell you about one season in late 1996 that stands out in my memory as a manifestation of the many-hued but closely woven coat of many colors. It happened during the 40 days of meetings called Houston Prayer Mountain.

UNITING FOR PRAYER AND WORSHIP

Although Houston rests on flat terrain, at one time there was an amphitheater overlooking the city. It was built on a man-made hill at the intersection of two major highways. It became the setting of a significant gathering for the Church in Houston, so called because the book of Revelation, recorded by the apostle John, addresses the churches of the New Testament as being represented within their cities—the Church in Ephesus, the Church in Smyrna, and so on.

Great expectancy arose in the leaders of the Church of Houston as we committed ourselves to join together for a time of corporate repentance and renewal. The first weekend of Houston Prayer Mountain took place in March 1996. We believed the timing was right for a major spiritual breakthrough in the city.

On the first day of Houston Prayer Mountain in November 1996, three hundred pastors and ministry leaders took communion together. We met for 40 nights of prayer and worship. Many of us fasted. We left our differences behind and came together for a common purpose—to worship the Lord and pray for souls. Nightly the front of the meeting place was filled as people came forward and God cleansed their hearts. Services often lasted five to six hours or more.

On one particular evening, a time for reconciliation took place. Restoration of relationships was happening at many of the gatherings, but this night was especially memorable. We spontaneously began to ask the Lord to show us if there were any barriers among us—any prejudices or hurts between members of different races or denominations that we needed to release.

Ministry leaders began to embrace and pray for one another. Christian Arab hugged messianic Jew, and Jew embraced German. Chinese and Japanese leaders prayed for each other. Anglo and African-American sought each other out. Mainline denominational and nondenominational ministers joined together in the essentials of the faith. Black, yellow, red, white and brown—a coat of many colors—was woven together that night. This was not planned; rather, it was a spontaneous work of God's Spirit. What an awesome sight to witness the healing that took place!

As we brought together people from different denominations and backgrounds, we recognized a common denominator: a passion for God and compassion for souls. We all desired to see souls added to God's kingdom. We prayed and fasted for this purpose.

One evening, 27 different nationalities attended the meeting. Many New Age and other religious people, drawn by the integration, were saved.

Thirty different worship teams, representing various denominations, races and cultures, eventually participated in Houston Prayer Mountain's praise and worship. The Lord blended the sounds into a sweet melody as inner-city ministries worshiped with those from suburban churches; front-line outreaches such as homeless shelters, AIDS ministries, inner-city youth ministries and gang ministries, all bridged their differences. The diversity was an expression of the beauty of the Bride of Christ.

Not only did we agree on a common purpose—evangelism—but we took action. What good is it to develop new concepts if we don't move from theory to practice? In one day alone, we distributed 80,000 pounds of food at a citywide feeding event, cooperating with Goad International. At another event, in cooperation with Operation Blessing, we gave away groceries to 5,000 families.

After the original 40 days of Houston Prayer Mountain, we gathered there again for five days around Easter weekend of 1997. Our final season of prayer at the amphitheater took place from December 26, 1997, and continued through February 1998. Then the owners of the facility closed it, and the hill upon which the amphitheater rested was leveled. Ironically, the amphitheater was replaced with a tree and plant nursery—a permanent reminder of all the spiritual seeds that took root and sprouted among us during the Houston Prayer Mountain services.

GOD WANTS TO WRAP US WITH HIS LOVE—HIS ROBE OF RIGHTEOUSNESS—SO THAT TOGETHER WE CAN BECOME A COAT OF MANY COLORS OFFERED BACK TO HIM.

The Lord humbled us and broke down many barriers during those days at Houston Prayer Mountain. Our time together was a small picture of what we read in Micah, as people gathered from various languages, nations and denominations from across the city. We realized that God wants to wrap us with His love—His robe of righteousness—so that together we can become a coat of many colors offered back to our Lord Jesus Christ. And He wants us to make a difference in the lives of others.

LAYING DOWN OUR LIVES AND PREJUDICES

When you and I put on Christ, we must also put on love (see Col. 3:14). Jesus displayed His love in dying for us while we were still sinners (see Rom. 5:8). He willingly chose to lay down His life for all nations, all peoples and all cultures. We did not earn or deserve His love, but Christ chose to love us anyway.

Because He did that for us, whatever offenses or prejudices we hold must be released. Some of the unforgiveness harbored may have been picked up from years past—within a particular church denomination or with someone of a particular racial background—yet we must get past these offenses if we want to impact our communities.

When I think of the embittered rage and offense many Christians today feel toward the gay community, I wonder how many of us would have hated Kenny. His story is a testimony against those whose prejudice would prevent them from ministry to homosexuals.

Kenny desperately wanted to end what was an unfulfilling lifestyle that always craved something more but was never satisfied. The men he lived with had money, expensive clothes and luxury apartments. They threw parties with designer drugs, fine wines and the best cuisine. Kenny struggled with his lust for that lifestyle, with its strings attached, and with his desire for the true freedom that he knew only came through Christ.

Kenny had been saved years earlier while in prison for robbery. He had committed the break-in to get money to pay bills but had spent what he took on drugs. The youngest son of an abusive father, he had been molested by both male and female baby-sitters while growing up. His parents divorced; then his father died. His mother moved in with an alcoholic whom Kenny hated. When he was 15, he became involved in drugs, which made it easy to experiment with homosexuality. The partying lifestyle took him straight to jail before he was out of his teens.

After his salvation in prison, Kenny never told anyone about his homosexual struggle. Upon his release, he served in a discipleship organization, his past firmly behind him. Then one night Kenny found himself with a man and was shocked that he could fall so easily. He became discouraged and fell for the lie that he was missing out on something by having left his previous lifestyle. He left his ministry involvement and became a waiter at a restaurant with friends who seemed to promise the excitement he'd been missing.

One night, Deborah, a girl who had been witnessing to Kenny, took him to a Bible study at my apartment. There I met Kenny for the first time. He felt the tug to join us, but instead moved into a gay apartment complex and began to feel he was beyond help. One of his friends was an embezzler and together they partied away the rewards of the embezzler's crime. I didn't see Kenny again for years.

Some time later, Kenny decided to get an HIV test for his own peace of mind. The results were positive. The test results seemed like an official death notice, but Kenny's lifestyle had beaten the disease to the punch. He felt dead inside. One lonely night he lay on his couch and whispered, "Lord, it's obvious I can't run my life. Help me."

A few weeks later he went out drinking with some friends when suddenly, sitting in a gay bar, he felt that he had to put down his beer and get out of there. When he walked outside, a Hispanic Turning Pointer stopped Kenny to give him a tract. Having experienced discrimination himself, this man felt no discrimination against a homosexual who needed Jesus. As a result, another life was snatched out of hell's gaping mouth.

There is a desperate need for healing in our land today. Our nation's citizens come from many cultural backgrounds and at times there have been serious conflicts to overcome. In a similar way, those in the Church come from different cultures, backgrounds and neighborhoods; but we are now one family with one common identity.

Within the Somebody Cares ministry, individuals represent many different nationalities and cultures. When I look around the room during our weekly services, I thank the Lord for each one He has brought there. Our worship team is even called "The Coat of Many Colors," for it is comprised of people from Asian, African-American, Jewish, Hispanic and Anglo backgrounds. We did not seek to have a racially mixed group, but each one was drawn by having the same heart for the Lord and a desire to see souls added to His kingdom.

CROSSING EVERY BOUNDARY

Because the kingdom of God is transcultural, He may send you to another nation, or He may ask you to go across town to work with people of a different background. Are you willing to go where He leads you? When you think of reaching out to particular groups or neighborhoods, what fears come to mind? We use a variety of excuses for not reaching out to others. Perhaps these comments sound familiar:

"I can't go into that neighborhood; they won't listen to me."

"You don't understand. I'm too old to talk with those people."

"I don't really want to go out in public with people like that."

"I can't talk to the checkout people at the supermarket or they'll think I'm a freak."

God is not limited by cultural, racial or denominational backgrounds, nor should we limit ourselves. It's not a Hispanic thing, an Asian thing, an African thing or an Anglo thing. It's a Jesus thing! God wants to use us to penetrate every neighborhood and every heart for His kingdom. But first we must deal with our own fears and prejudices and then make ourselves available. We could be the very ones to bring about healing and breakthrough for others.

TOGETHER ON FIRE

A picture hangs in my office: Jesus wearing a vibrant tunic covered with national flags from all over the world. On several occasions, in some measure, this picture became a reality in our city. One of those occasions was the Together on Fire gathering, which brought together different Asian ethnicities.

The gathering, coordinated by Joy Wong, and assisted by Somebody Cares Houston's pastors, was a breathtaking experience unprecedented in Houston history at the time. Both evenings began with a procession of national flags. Forming a circle at the altar, each minister bowed his flag as the cross of Christ was raised high above them all. We took Communion together, acknowledging that though nations may have been divided in the past, they were now united through the gospel of Christ.

Across the front of the sanctuary, the national flags provided a backdrop for two extraordinary services. Pastors took the platform, displaying the beauty of their cultures through native costumes that represented the communities of Vietnamese, Chinese, Taiwanese, Japanese, Indian, Filipino, Korean, Indonesian, Hispanic, Jewish and African peoples. Each prayed in his or her native tongue for revival in our city and in their homelands.

Houston is second only to New York for diversity of cultures and languages spoken. That first night, racial and cultural barriers fell as the Church of Houston stood united to reach the lost. I had the privilege of sharing an evangelistic challenge both evenings, and many came to the altar to receive Christ. From teen to adult, lives were changed forever.

Pastor Kim of the Korean Christian Church of Houston said, "I saw a definite awareness that our local church is not the end of our mission, but our mission is to see revival come to all nations. It was also a joy to hear the different prayers in their native languages, especially the Hebrew prayer. When the messianic rabbi prayed in Hebrew, I saw the Old and New Testaments come together, with the Old Testament being fulfilled in the New. It was awesome."

Think of the impact the Church in any city will have if all races and denominations unify in order to win the lost! This is the Lord's desire and will bring great joy to His heart. Picture the threads of the coat blending into a tapestry of all national flags as we, Christ's Church, become one Body.

Houston missed out on a great visitation by God in the early years of the twentieth century. A black preacher named William Seymour came to Houston, but was not allowed to participate in the Bible classes except on the other side of a screen that separated the races. He eventually left Houston and went to Los Angeles—where he was instrumental in sparking the Azusa Street revival that reached millions. Because of racial prejudice, our city missed out on a visitation of God.

We believe that God wants to bring a mighty revival to the land, and we don't want to miss it. One of our slogans in the city is "Give us Houston, give us the nation."

THE UNFINISHED COAT OF MANY COLORS

Remember the story of our Hispanic Turning Pointer who handed a tract to a homosexual desperate to find a way out of his lifestyle? That one simple action eventually brought Kenny into God's kingdom to add his color to the robe. It took months to break down the walls Kenny had built in his life. But eventually, alone in his apartment, he reached out and touched his Bible for the first time in years. He knew how to repent and how to pray. That night he felt life surge within him again, and soon he joined us to grow and learn.

Kenny started taking missions trips to Mexico, Central and South America and Europe. His HIV was slow to progress, and his strength was slow to fail. On his second trip to Germany, he fell in love with the German people, and he travels there often, making a difference for Christ in that country. Who would have dreamed that handing a tract—just a piece of paper—to a man emerging from a homosexual nightclub was part of the Lord's plan to birth a missionary?

Where is God challenging you to go? To the streets? To your neighborhood? To the schools, the government or to another nation? Find out where the people in your community are going. What do they do to deal with their hurts? Where do they run? We must follow them and identify their real needs so we can be instruments of God's healing.

Our faithfulness to the Lord today is an important step in fulfilling His long-range call on our lives. He has not finished weaving His coat of many colors. He will not be finished until every last soul has an opportunity to respond to the gospel. That is the challenge set before us.

CHAPTER FOUR

"Launch out into the deep and let down your nets for a catch." But Simon answered and said to Him, "Master, we have toiled all night and caught nothing; nevertheless at Your word I will let down the net." And when they had done this, they caught a great number of fish, and their net was breaking. So they signaled to their partners in the other boat to come and help them. And they came and filled both the boats, so that they began to sink.

LUKE 5:4-7

MENDING THE NET

Imagine the thoughts that went through Simon Peter's mind when Jesus told him to cast his net again after a whole night of catching no fish: *I've been working at this a long time. I've already put my net in the water but haven't caught anything. Why would the results be any different this time?*

Peter wrestled with his doubts, yet he obeyed Jesus and put the net in the water on the other side of the boat. Peter walked in faith, trusting that the Lord knew better than he did. Sure enough, the net was soon filled with fish. In fact, the net was so full that Peter had to call his neighbors to help him.

What joy must have filled Peter's heart! Yet the event also left him shaken: "When Simon Peter saw it, he fell down at Jesus' knees, saying, 'Depart from me, for I am a sinful man, O Lord!' For he and all who were with him were astonished at the catch of fish which they had taken" (Luke 5:8,9).

The disciples' labor through the night is like our labor in the flesh. Very little is accomplished by our own efforts, but when the Lord directs us, that's when we see results. Jesus spoke the word; the disciples obeyed and then pulled in a multitude of fish.

Nothing is greater than seeing the hand of God intervene in a situation.

Like Peter, we are called to be fishers of men. There is no shortage of fish. Millions of people are waiting to be brought into the kingdom. The question is, How can we bring in the greatest catch? We routinely cast our fishing hooks into the water—with friendship evangelism, crusades and church services—but we don't catch the greatest number of fish with those individual approaches. If our approach to fishing yields few results, or if the fish we catch do not stay caught, then it's time to change what we're doing.

A single fishing pole does catch one fish at a time. But with a net we can bring in many fish at once. Although we are called individually to a particular area of ministry, collectively we are called to the world. As we tie our individual abilities and ministries together, we can bring in the catch God has prepared.

SPREAD, WASH AND CAST THE NET

What were the fishermen doing when Jesus first approached them? "But the fishermen had gone from them [the boats] and were washing their nets" (Luke 5:2). To prepare for fishing, the nets were first spread out and then washed. Likewise, we must open our nets first by opening our hearts and allowing the Lord to cleanse us and deal with any issues—insecurities, fears or hurts from the past—that hinder His work through us.

When Dennis and Mary came to our Turning Point services from another church, they were fearful of allowing themselves to hook up with us, or with any Christians, for that matter. I soon learned why. They had been part of the "shepherding move-ment," which taught that people must have accountability to leadership. Taken to the extreme, as in their case, leaders and elders controlled every decision.

Mary had never trusted the leadership of the church, but Dennis believed they were good people who wanted to do right. After many years of being shepherded to the extent that others even told Dennis what job he could have and what car he could buy, one day he learned of some financial misdealings in the leadership and was crushed.

Mary had recently heard me talk at a Bible study about the Church in Vietnam, and she was intrigued enough to suggest to Dennis that they come hear me together. Dennis felt apprehen-sive. He'd been so shattered that he believed he could never again be part of the Body of Christ or trust anyone in church leadership.

When I heard their story, I urged Dennis and Mary to come and hang out with us, but I didn't ask them to do anything. You see, until the "net" of their lives had been spread out, opened up and cleaned, there was no reason to put it to work in the boat. They weren't ready. But God's love and His Word worked over a period of time and they overcame their hurts and fears. Both Dennis and Mary experienced pain in the healing process, but it was also a time of character building.

It took them a while to get used to the fact that I wasn't going to tell them what to do. Instead, I was going to teach them how to hear God's voice for themselves. After many months,

Dennis and Mary finally felt ready to jump into the boat and be part of the mended net for the Church of Houston. When they did, they watched the Lord draw people to Himself.

A Mended Net

After the nets are spread out and washed, they are placed back in the boat, ready to be used for the catch. Jesus instructed the disciples, "Launch out into the deep and let down your nets for a catch" (Luke 5:4). He used the word "nets" as if they had not one net but many. In the next verse Peter agrees to let down "the net," singular. Could it be that the fishermen had connected their nets into one large net? By faith, were they anticipating a great catch? They cast the net into the water, "and when they had done this, they caught a great number of fish, and their net was breaking" (v. 6).

When Peter and the disciples obeyed the Lord, the one net was neither large enough nor strong enough to hold all the fish. What were they to do? Their resources were limited, and they had nothing else with which to catch the fish. Peter had to act quickly, or they would lose the fish. "So they signaled to their partners in the other boat to come and help them. And they came and filled both the boats, so that they began to sink" (v. 7).

The disciples learned a valuable principle that day. They needed the help of other fishermen to bring in the catch. No single person, church or ministry working alone can handle the harvest of souls the Lord desires to bring into His kingdom. Our focus is not on building individual kingdoms but on building God's kingdom. To see His kingdom built, we must be willing to link our net with the nets of others for an even greater catch.

We who are fishers of men often face times of discouragement when it seems that the labor is in vain. Each of us goes through seasons when the fruit is hard to harvest, and we find ourselves tempted to go back to our old ways. After Jesus died, the disciples grieved their loss and went back to what they did before they met Him:

> Simon Peter said to them, "I am going fishing." They said to him, "We are going with you also." They went out and immediately got into the boat, and that night they caught nothing (John 21:3).

Jesus appeared to them after the Resurrection and instructed them,

> "Cast the net on the right side of the boat, and you will find some." So they cast, and now they were not able to draw it in because of the multitude of fish. Simon Peter went up and dragged the net to land, full of large fish, one hundred and fifty-three; and although there were so many, the net was not broken (John 21:6,11).

MANY EVANGELISTIC MINISTRIES HAVE BEEN TORN UP WHILE TRYING TO DRAW IN THEIR NETS, NOT REALIZING THERE IS SYNERGY AND SAFETY IN PARTNERING WITH OTHERS.

That's when the disciples worked together to drag the net to shore. As they combined their efforts, they successfully brought in the catch, and the net was not even torn. Many evangelistic ministries have been torn up while trying to draw in their nets, not realizing there is synergy and safety in partnering with others.

Scripture says that Peter and his friends in the neighboring boats brought in 153 fish, a number that theologians say represents the known nations at that time in history. Even by the number of fish caught, Jesus prophetically spoke to the disciples and to us with the message that we will make disciples of all peoples, tribes, tongues and nations.

Though the disciples had gone back to fishing, Jesus was reminding them of their original calling: "I will make you become fishers of men" (Mark 1:17). The calling had never changed. Though circumstances spoke a contrary message, Jesus was telling them that His purpose would be fulfilled in their lives.

The same is true for us. Though the night has been long and the catch has been small, God's plan never changes. He will instruct us how to bring in the harvest; and though the net is filled, it will not break. He will faithfully watch over us and assist us in becoming fishers of men.

As a result of Somebody Cares Houston linking nets for a greater catch, we are reaching the community at a grassroots level. We maintain our distinctiveness and our individual callings, but we recognize that we need to work together to see a vast number of people reached. This takes some doing, but the work is so worthwhile that the time involved and the price paid cannot be compared to the joy of seeing lives changed by Christ.

Although God is already doing a great work within separate ministries, the next step is to link the ministries together to become part of something bigger than ourselves. As we become a mended net, even with our diversities and our distinctiveness, we can reach a greater harvest.

United We Stand

God has a plan for each of us once we are cleaned and mended and ready to link with others. Dennis and Mary eventually went to the Willie George children's ministry in Tulsa to intern for two years. They returned to Turning Point and became our children's pastors, which includes participating in the larger outreach to children of our community through Somebody Cares. Upon graduation, several churches and ministries offered them lucrative jobs, which they turned down to return to Houston. Dennis and Mary wanted to serve as missionaries to the children under the umbrella of Somebody Cares Houston, and they have remained focused and faithful to that calling.

Jesus reminded the disciples of their first calling and responsibility when He told them they would be fishers of men. That's what we are, too. As we cast our nets and work with our neighbors, we will have the greatest possible catch without breaking the net. A true network is a net that works.

CHAPTER FIVE

Jerusalem shall be inhabited as towns without walls, because of the multitude of men and livestock in it. "For I," says the LORD, "will be a wall of fire all around her, and I will be the glory in her midst."

ZECHARIAH 2:4,5

UNITY WITH A PURPOSE

The young man, drenched with water, laid his head on Pastor Lopez's shoulder and embraced him. He had found hope and newness of life that day and the baptism sealed the work God had done. His was one of many testimonies that came out of a citywide baptism held at an entertainment water park. Water park officials said we had a record attendance of 4,100 people. This was another memorable day for Houston as denominational and racial walls came down for a common focus. We were united for a purpose that would have eternal consequences.

Richard Hinojosa, youth pastor of the Encourager Church, and I preached from a platform in the wave pool. Over 100 churches took part, and close to 50 pastors representing many denominations and ethnicities helped baptize over 600 people.

One pastor knelt down in the water as he prayed for a young boy before baptizing him. Some jumped out of the water filled with joy. Young adults committed to walk radically and boldly in purity with Christ. One young teen raised his arms, fists clenched, giving a victory punch as he rose from the water. A woman shook her arms in praise as she was baptized.

Small prayer huddles comprised of young and old joined hands and prayed with the same heart cry. Throughout the baptisms, individuals continued to ask for prayer to receive Christ. By conservative estimates, 200 people made first-time commitments or rededications to Christ.

That day spiritual chains broke off people's lives and the battle was won for souls! Of the shades of black, white, yellow and brown, only one color was seen that day—blood red! You could sense the freedom and victory Jesus brought.

Local television networks filmed and reported the city-wide baptism. Our local NBC station reported, "Hundreds of Houstonians turned out for a big baptism at Adventure Bay Water Theme Park. Houston area pastors and ministers from various denominations did the honors for this celebration of Christian faith." The historic impact of the day came from the power of God and was far beyond anything we had imagined.

IT IS VERY GOOD

The work each ministry is sowing into our city is good. But when we unite, the results go beyond good to tremendous.

During Houston Prayer Mountain, Pastor Glenn Carter, who has served on the Somebody Cares Houston advisory committee, was a guest on a local television station. He shared about his involvement in Somebody Cares and explained how each participating ministry is important to God. He made a parallel between our networking of ministries and the creation story from Genesis one. "And God saw that it was good. . . . Then God saw everything that He had made, and indeed it was very good" (Gen. 1:10,31). After day one, God looked at His creation and said, "It is good." After the second, third, fourth and fifth days, He looked at His creation and said, "It is very good."

Reflecting on Pastor Glenn's comments, I, too, believe that the Father looks at each denomination, each inner-city ministry, each suburban church and says, "It is good." Yet as we work together with a common purpose, I sense Him saying, "It is very good." Individually each ministry is good and is doing a good work. But as one united body we are effective in bringing in a great harvest that is pleasing to the Father.

Jim Herrington, currently the director of Mission Houston, and I have become friends. One day while having lunch together, he said, "The reason I can be a part of Somebody Cares is because you've never asked me to give up my personal distinction."

The leaders in Houston appreciate each other's distinctiveness and appreciate the manner in which the Lord is using each individual or ministry to build His kingdom. No one asks others to give up their individual callings. That is why Somebody Cares works. Synergy takes place in the presence of a noncompetitive servant attitude that desires to build the Lord's kingdom as opposed to man's kingdom. We each bring what we have to the table and see what the Lord would have us do.

When Jim was interviewed by the *Houston Chronicle* in 1996 for an article about Somebody Cares, he told them that the network is bringing together "a broad range of ministries who are touching people that traditional churches are not touching. It is street people, teenagers and Generation Xers who don't find traditional church to have any meaning for them. Moreover, [we are] successfully reflecting the worldwide trend of churches and ministries to unite or cooperate for more effective ministry."

This is the purpose of the Somebody Cares unity. We do not advocate ecumenical unity, which is merely unity for unity's sake. Rather, we unite with a purpose.

Reaching Out to Bring Them In

Working together is the start. Gaining a shared vision for your city is the next step. Your ability to make an impact is directly related to how much you love your city and how much you believe God wants to do great things there.

Ethel Dunn, known as Mama, is an African-American woman who provides a homeless shelter in downtown Houston called God's Little Lighthouse. When God got hold of her heart, Ethel sold her business in Alaska and moved to Houston to help the needy. She became involved in Somebody Cares through Houston Prayer Mountain and the ministers she met there. As relationships grew, some ministries offered to help at the shelter. Churches provided volunteers. Others provided workers and supplies to remove six layers of shingles and put on a new roof. Not only was Ethel's ministry blessed, but everyone who served with her was enriched.

Ray Highfield is the founder and director of His Touch Ministries, a home for those with HIV and AIDS. Our heart goes out to Ray and his staff as they provide care and counseling every single day to residents and those who call. We were privileged to join His Touch Ministries for a Concert of Praise in which other area churches provided workers and raised community awareness. Ray is now traveling extensively, teaching AIDS awareness and prompting Christian communities nationwide to create outreaches to those affected by AIDS in their communities. The Church is becoming the tangible extension of Christ's love as we address these serious needs.

The Amazing Fruit of Synergy

What would it be like if the churches and ministries in your city worked together in a network similar to that of Somebody Cares, not just for a specific project but as a long-term commitment? Your city would never be the same. This is more than a theory—it has been tested and proven in our ongoing experience in Houston. It has spread to Southern California, to Tampa Bay, Florida, to Denver, Colorado, and elsewhere around the nation and the world.

Just in Houston alone we have distributed over 150,000 Somebody Cares New Testaments citywide, plus the Spanish equivalent, Alguien Se Interesa. In 1996, 40 million pounds of food were distributed by Action Ministries, working in conjunction with Somebody Cares. In 1997 that figure rose to 102 million pounds of food. By 1999, 115 million pounds of food were distributed!

Last year at Christmas, someone gave us retail space in one of the local malls and we distributed 10,600 toys to underserved children who were able to take a trip to the mall to pick out their Christmas presents just like more advantaged children. Including this outreach, we created several hundred Somebody Cares bears, which were the most coveted toy of all—little plush white bears wearing a T-shirt with the same message as the business card, "A true witness rescues lives" and our website address.

One year, we rotated a billboard around the city with the message "Area churches and ministries want you to know Somebody Cares Houston." Currently, we have several billboards around the city displaying the same message. Another year we partnered with CBN and distributed over a half million copies of *Book of Hope*. We offered prayer door hangers, which we distributed to over 1 million homes. We also obtained the rights to air the movie *Resurrection* for one year and aired it on both secular and Christian television stations.

AS WE WORK TOGETHER AND PRAY TOGETHER, WE INCREASINGLY RECOGNIZE THAT WE DO NOT REPRESENT INDIVIDUAL MINISTRIES BUT THE BODY OF CHRIST IN OUR CITY.

Synergy works wherever people are willing to unite. Somebody Cares Southland in the Los Angeles area has burst into life. In the year 2000, Somebody Cares Southland distributed over $4 million worth of food and mobilized thousands of prayer warriors statewide; worked with a dozen communities to air the *Jesus* video and taught hundreds of volunteers on evangelism; coordinated youth prayer events and conducted Care Days in needy areas with live music, free food and ministry; and distributed roughly 60,000 toys at Christmas. In addition, they networked with ministries from Lowell Lundstrom to Lighthouses of Prayer to Operation Blessing and coordinated with hundreds of local churches.

Unseen things done for the Kingdom are just as important and are helping the overall effort to reach the lost. One night, while ministering at an inner-city church, I had the privilege of meeting a woman who has been praying for revival in our city for more than 20 years. God has heard her prayers. He honors those hours she and so many like her have spent on their knees and the tears they have wept for souls. They have prepared the way for revival.

A Hunger for Revival

As we work together and pray for each other, we increasingly recognize that we do not represent individual ministries but the Body of Christ in our city. In Houston, during monthly pastors' meetings, we take the opportunity to pray for ministers who are coming into the city or are being sent out from the city. In this way, we acknowledge as city elders that we will cover them in prayer in addition to the covering of their local church and give them a corporate blessing from the Church of Houston.

One couple received a vision at Houston Prayer Mountain and left our ministry to serve in Asia, so several Houston pastors prayed over them. As the elders of the city, we sent them out with a blessing and covering. Another minister had served as an associate pastor of a local church, then was asked to become the senior pastor. First, we blessed the pastor who was leaving the position and prayed for continued fruitfulness and favor in his life; and then we prayed for the new pastor and his wife. On behalf of the Church of Houston, we received them into their new position. In such ways, we endeavor to serve the local congregation and further its ties with the Body of Christ in our city.

Ultimately we are representing Christ. But wherever the Lord may send us, we are also representing the Church of our city. We want to be ambassadors about whom the Lord and others will give a good report.

Pastor Lopez, who worked with us at the baptism, has since expanded his men's and women's homes, moved into new facilities, strengthened their work to gang members and has become a regional pastor for the Victory Outreach churches in the area. Picture him with the other ministers at one of our monthly Somebody Cares Houston meetings. He arrives along with the young and the old, every race and denomination, those helping the homeless, ex-convicts, recovering addicts, unwed moms and street kids.

At such meetings, we come together to seek the Lord for revival in our communities, our city and our nation. The love of God transcends our differences, and warm fellowship envelopes us as we discuss strategies to reach our city. We minister to one another, share our individual visions and present practical needs. We feel privileged to serve alongside men and women who are making a difference in people's lives. We appreciate each other, but none of us wants to be the other. We don't compete for another's ministry.

SPARKS FROM HOUSTON

Several years ago I envisioned the outpouring God desires to bring to our city and the world. I saw little flickers of flames, representing the intercessors, the churches and the Christian communities that have been praying for revival. The flickers of flame lit across the greater Houston area and, as a wind began to blow, the flickers spread into a huge fire. From that fire, embers went out across the nation and to other countries. As God's Spirit blows through the city, the impact on Houston will spread outward to the nations.

Flames of revival and renewal are meant to rekindle that which has died. Do we hunger and thirst for God's righteousness to consume us and then sweep across our land?

God desires to burn a fire that ignites flames of revival in our cities. Like a raging forest fire, these revival flames will become uncontrollable. They will not be isolated to a particular area but will engulf the entire nation. "'For I,' says the LORD, 'will be a wall of fire all around her, and I will be the glory in her midst'" (Zech. 2:5). God's revival flames form a wall of protection; they refine as well as consume. Before the flames can go outward to consume our enemies, they must purify us, lest we, too, be consumed.

Toward the end of the 40 days on Houston Prayer Mountain, it was clear that something significant and unprecedented had taken place. Many requested we keep the meetings going, yet God spoke to me through another surprising vision. I saw a huge mountain, representing Houston Prayer Mountain, and then I saw a huge body of water, which represented the city of Houston. The mountain crumbled and disappeared into the water, and as it did, the water level rose. I sensed that God was saying the mountain would die so the spiritual water level would rise throughout the city.

On the last night of Houston Prayer Mountain, we held a candlelight prayer service to act out physically what we saw spiritually. The flickers of candlelight represented the saints who have prayed to the Lord of the harvest. The little flickers united spread the flames of God's fire.

Instead of just a centralized revival, the Lord wants the sparks of revival to set churches ablaze in every area of the city. We are now beginning to see a dynamic taking place that is indeed drawing people from other cities and nations. God is blowing His wind to ignite our flickers into revival flames.

When Steve Riggle, pastor of Grace Community Church in Houston's Clear Lake City, commented on Houston Prayer

Mountain, he said, "Prayer Mountain was a catalyst for our city in revival, at least in my estimation. Our church is radically changed; the focus of our church and outreaches has changed considerably. I think of what will take place, not knowing how the whole process will unfold. But I believe what we've seen so far is just a small beginning."

The Blue Heelers
A Modern-Day Parable

Hank Marion, pastor of Bammel Baptist Church, serves on the Somebody Cares Houston steering committee. He has traveled with us to other cities to communicate the vision and strategies of Somebody Cares. He tells this story that illustrates the message of unity with a purpose.

My dad has property in East Texas with 100 cows. Three times a year all the cows are gathered into a corral to receive care. The process of getting the cows into the corral is not easy. Cows are not like dogs and cats that come running when you call them. In fact they seem to sense when we are having a roundup and run to the far side of the ranch.

My dad's friend has blue heelers, which are called "cow dogs." They are bred and trained to herd the cows into the corral. Whenever possible, we contact our friend with the dogs to get him involved in our roundup. Typically, at 7 A.M., we gather at the corral and greet each other while sharing stories and sipping coffee. At the appropriate time, the owner of the blue heelers will walk over to the cages and open the doors, while giving a shout: "Go get 'em."

Like lightning those dogs take off. This is what they live for, and nothing keeps them from the task. Across the pasture they bolt and surround the cows. Then with precision and teamwork they bring the cows up the hill through all the gates and into the corral.

One time, another friend who lives just up the road was planning his own roundup. He knew about the blue heelers and invited them to come and work his cows, but there was one problem: instead of 100 cows, this man had about 500 cows. The owner of the blue heelers knew this was too much for his dogs to handle, but he had three friends who also had blue heelers. They decided they would all bring their dogs over on roundup day.

So there we were about 7 A.M., and it came time to let the dogs out. The owners did just that, but much to our surprise the dogs ran to each other instead of taking off after the cows. They walked around each other sniffin' and snarlin' and checking each other out. Their masters were yelling at the top of their voices, "Blue, git on," and "Beau, stop it now." But it wasn't until the dogs decided everything was okay that they ran down the hill into the pasture and brought the cows into the pen.

The Lord has a big job for us to do. The harvest He has planned is so huge that it is going to require the whole Church to accomplish it. He desires that we work together instead of separately. We must get past the sniffin' and snarlin' and become comfortable with one another. Otherwise, when the job is at hand and the work has begun we will waste precious time.

We have to look at the need in the field—the mighty harvest waiting—and get over the sniffin' and snarlin' and growlin'. We must humble ourselves and work together to build God's kingdom.

Is this not the fast that I have chosen: to loose the bonds of wickedness, to undo the heavy burdens, to let the oppressed go free, and that you break every yoke? Is it not to share your bread with the hungry, and that you bring to your house the poor who are cast out; when you see the naked, that you cover him, and not hide yourself from your own flesh? Then your light shall break forth like the morning, your healing shall spring forth speedily, and your righteousness shall go before you; the glory of the LORD shall be your rear guard. Then you shall call, and the LORD will answer; you shall cry, and He will say, "Here I am."

I S A I A H   5 8 : 6 - 9

PRAYING AND FASTING WITH A PURPOSE

Turning Point's "fried chicken bandit" spent a total of eight months in the free world between Christmas 1969 and July 1985. Bob Camp was charged with armed robbery of a Kentucky Fried Chicken store, aggravated assault, possession of heroin, felony theft and a dozen other charges that put him in jail three different times. Each time he was released, he returned within four months.

During what would become Bob's final prison sentence, his drug-addicted brother, Ray, stumbled into a Christian bookstore in search of help. One of our original Turning Pointers, Randy Flinn, felt God tell him to go help a man in that same Christian bookstore. Just as Ray was looking at a row of Bibles and silently praying, "God if you are real, I need a sign," Randy walked up and said, "Do you need some help?"

After Ray's conversion, Bob was released from prison. He had met the Lord years earlier at a prayer meeting during the "Jesus-freak" movement and had thrown his drugs out the car window of a friend, whose brother had taken them to the prayer meeting. None of the three continued to follow Christ.

A friend took Bob to a church and to a Narcotics Anonymous meeting, but Bob wasn't going to return to Christ easily. For eight years he screamed, cussed and growled at people in his NA and AA meetings. He was diagnosed with manic depression, but prescribed drugs couldn't control him. He didn't want to go to prison again, so he stayed off drugs and alcohol and continued to struggle with his thoughts and emotions.

At a checkup during a hot July day in 1992, Bob's doctor told him he'd be on lithium for the rest of his life—news that sent him to the breaking point. When he drove his truck away from the doctor's office, he thought he heard a page and called a number on his pager.

"Can I help you?" he asked the person on the other line, indicating to the listener that he was answering his pager.

"I didn't page anyone," said a man's voice.

"Well, I'm Bob Camp, a roofing contractor. Is there anything I can do for you?"

"Well, I'm a pastor, and I lead people to the Lord. Is there anything I can do for you?"

Bob doesn't remember the man's prayer, but he remembers going to his AA meeting that night and telling them God had called him on the telephone that day.

A friend from AA invited him to a Turning Point meeting, and that night, Bob responded to the altar call. Bob now says that I gave him the creeps that night. Bob's terminology meant that the presence of the Holy Spirit was making him uncomfortable. He came up to me after the service and said, "You must be saying something pretty heavy because I can't understand a word of it." I just responded, "Keep coming."

His AA friend then took Bob to a local church, and that is where the breakthrough came. Bob believed that since he'd been saved years earlier, he didn't need to answer the call for salvation. But something during the altar call stirred him inside. He started to shake. The pastor said, "There's one more person who should answer the call tonight, and if you don't, you're going to regret it tomorrow."

Bob's first thought was to run out of the church, but instead he went to the front. As the pastor prayed with those at the altar, he said to Bob, "Tell Satan to leave you."

"Please leave me," Bob said.

"No, command him," the pastor said.

Bob didn't need a lot of encouragement to get angry. He shocked the entire church when he started screaming, "In the name of Jesus, get out of me NOW!"

The next time Bob entered one of our meetings, I could see the difference in him immediately. He was not only saved, he was delivered.

The Lord desires that none should perish but that all would come to the saving knowledge of His Son, Jesus Christ (see 2 Pet. 3:9). He cares for the lost and wants to use us to lead them to a relationship with Him. Wimpy prayers won't bring deliverance to those enslaved by Satan. We must pray—individually and corporately—and pray with a purpose, asking, "God, what would You have me do?"

The two friends with whom Bob was originally saved as a young man returned to Christ, one in his final days before dying of AIDS. God desires to save and deliver every prison inmate, drug addict and hopeless case. Our part is to pray for them.

WALLS COME DOWN

A well-known saying of Dr. Edwin Louis Cole is that "we become intimate with the One to whom we pray, the one with whom we pray and the one for whom we pray." From our place of intimacy with God, we become sensitive to His heart and His concerns, and we become intimate with others.

No evangelism can take place without a foundation of prayer. More than pious religious incantations, the prayer we need to pray is one of desperate, heartrending, passionate intercession. Missionary John Hyde modeled this when he cried out to God, "Give me souls or I die!" It was also exemplified by Bob Pierce, founder of World Vision, who prayed, "Break my heart with the things that break Yours."

Many avenues exist for individual and corporate prayer. I found one while seeking the Lord for His strategy in the early 1980s. I felt directed to the book of Joshua, and as I read about Joshua's march around the walled city of Jericho, something lit up inside me. Though the concept was not popular at the time, a group of Turning Pointers implemented Jericho Marches around the environs of Houston and specifically at secular rock concerts. Today, some refer to these marches as prayer walks.

We would walk and pray in advance of the event. During the event we would distribute gospel tracts and minister one-on-one as we walked and prayed. Many were added to the Kingdom as a result—some who are still working with us today.

After one concert, one young man wrote, "I read your Iron Maiden tract and said the prayer. It changed my life completely. I am asking for more tracts. Anything y'all have got I will pass around."

At another concert, a young woman was sick, and a group of young men were trying to take advantage of her. I challenged them, saying they were wimps, because real men would help her. Our group took her to the hospital, cared for her and led her to Christ. At the next concert, we were again witnessing outside when a young woman approached us to say she was hoping we'd be there. She had watched us help the sick woman at the previous concert and wanted to know about God.

Years later, at a church service, a young man approached me and said he was one of the young punks harassing the sick woman at that concert. He said he and his friends had intended to beat me up, but they were so intimidated when I called them wimps that they stood there just trying to maintain their dignity. Later he found a church and gave his heart to Christ.

Evangelism and prayer go hand in hand. Prayer is fundamental to our relationship with God; but from that place of prayer we move to a place of action. Evangelism is a natural result of our relationship with God.

Jericho Drives

Joshua and the Israelites set a precedent for us when they marched around the walls of Jericho (see Josh. 6). They obeyed the Lord's instruction and trusted Him to bring down the walls of the city.

In 1988, some Houston-area ministers asked me what I thought was the next step for the city. We discussed strategies to pull down barriers within the Church and see our city won for Christ. Though many wanted to see breakthroughs, it was clear that action was needed first within the Church if we were to see walls in the community come down. The pastors agreed that a

Jericho Drive and rally could bring an initial breakthrough in the Body of Christ as well as in the city.

The first Jericho Drive was held May 7, 1988. We drove seven times around a highway that encircles the city, praying against specific strongholds. We culminated the drive with a prayer rally.

The Jericho Drives continued annually for four years and they continue to occur spontaneously to this day. When they took place, once a day for six days we took turns driving around the highway that encircles the city. On the seventh day, we sometimes drove around the highway in shifts. But on the seventh time around, the entire group caravanned together, praying for souls. Each drive ended with a praise rally at a local church. Some area pastors now conduct all-night prayer meetings that conclude with a Jericho Drive for the city.

What seemed radical at the time are now common events worldwide. Intercessors and community prayer leaders frequently call for prayer walks and prayer drives exactly like the Jericho Drive we once did more out of inspiration than organization.

One prayer walk in particular stands out in my mind. In 1997, Kendall Bridges, pastor of The Worship Center Assembly of God, felt he was to fast for personal and corporate revival. In his own words, here is what happened:

What started as a 10-day fast was extended to 21 days and then to 40 days. A few men from our church joined me. After the fast, I experienced personal revival and we experienced revival in our church. A new depth of consecration developed. But I realized that if we want citywide revival, it is going to take consistent consecration and consistent sacrifice. We often make commitments leading up to special events, then go back to mediocrity afterward. Each of us has to make a deeper commitment. So, how bad do we want it?

In addition to the fast, God called those men and myself to a Jericho Walk for our city. We began at 8 P.M. one Friday night and walked the 610 Loop around downtown Houston, about a 40-mile walk. The next week, God moved on my heart to do another Jericho Walk around a larger loop, Beltway 8, which is almost 90 miles. In preparation, I faxed area churches and ministries and asked for their prayer requests, and we lifted those needs to the Lord while we walked.

The walk took four days, averaging 20 miles per day. We held nightly services, and I asked a different minister to share the Word each night. Ministers from Asian, Hispanic and African-American backgrounds participated. If we want to keep seeing revival, we must continue to sacrifice. Though I am not much into walking, getting out there and being alone with God was wonderful.

In addition to occasional prayer drives or prayer walks, we have ongoing organized prayer for our city. As their part in Somebody Cares, Pastor Emeritus Richard Shearer's staff at Bammel Baptist Church have implemented and continue to oversee a prayer activity called Occupy the Land. On a grid map of Houston, 2,700 square miles are broken into half-mile square sectors. Individuals from dozens of churches have adopted various segments for which they are committed to pray each day. Over 75 percent of this area is now covered by daily prayer. To have people praying for their neighborhoods daily has taken a major commitment, but it is a vital part of the harvest in our city.

DISCERNING SPIRITUAL STRONGHOLDS

In 1988, during the first Jericho Drive, Pastor Mike Cave of New Life Christian Center in Houston shared a message that is still pertinent today. He said:

> The changes taking place in cities today will either move them toward more evil, more corruption, or else something will intervene to reverse the trend and move the cities toward godliness. Whoever takes the lead in these major mega-centers of our world is going to affect the course of history. . . .
>
> People are drawn to the city with a false hope of security in jobs, in commerce and in all the things they mistakenly assume [it] will provide for them. In reality, the spirit of the city is nothing but a web that draws people into its clutches. The Church must intercede and cry out to God for mercy.

WHILE MEN REACH FOR THRONES TO BUILD THEIR OWN KINGDOMS, JESUS REACHED FOR A TOWEL TO WASH MEN'S FEET.

Because of the variety and number of people in Houston, there exists a variety of strongholds, including pride, greed, violence, moral impurity and a spirit of control that rebels against God's authority. An independent mentality has hindered the Church in our city and throughout the Body of Christ in America. For that reason, getting churches and ministries to work together is a difficult process. Yet breakthroughs come as area ministry leaders colabor for the sake of the lost.

Within Turning Point Ministries we teach young disciples a basic principle, which we pray they will carry with them to any church, ministry or mission field in which they serve. That principle is this: *While men reach for thrones to build their own kingdoms, Jesus reached for a towel to wash men's feet.* We must have a servant's heart toward each other and toward this generation. Only with this sacrificial attitude will we see the needed breakthroughs in the Church and in our cities, and souls added to God's kingdom.

REBUILDING SPIRITUAL WALLS

Prayer is not just talking to God, it is listening to His voice and being ready to obey. As we develop an intimate relationship with the Lord and with each other, we receive His corporate instruction to reach our communities and follow through with action.

We have more people praying for revival in America today than ever before. We are crying out to God and claiming the promise of Chronicles, that if we humble ourselves, pray, seek His face and turn from our wicked ways, He will hear from heaven and heal our land (see 2 Chron. 7:14). Yet we often forget the requirement Isaiah gave us to reach outward to the needy in addition to reaching upward to God. When we commit ourselves to both upward and outward thrusts, nothing can stop revival: "Then your light shall break forth like the morning, your healing shall spring forth speedily, and your righteousness shall go before you; the glory of the LORD shall be your rear guard" (Isa. 58:8).

John R. Mott was a great Protestant statesman and a 1946 Nobel laureate. Understanding the power of evangelism when combined with social action, Mott once remarked, "Evangelism without social work is deficient; social work without evangelism is impotent."[1] Separating these two components of effective outreach has been a tragic mistake of much of our evangelism in the past century.

God wants the spiritual walls of our city rebuilt, but this means more than devising an elaborate spiritual infrastructure; the real issue is rebuilding the lives of people shattered by the consequences of sin.

Bob Camp, the fried chicken bandit, became an integral part of our ministry. For years now he has led services in prisons and helped with pastoral care for new converts coming out of drug and alcohol. A few years after his salvation, God spoke to his heart at Houston Prayer Mountain about a young woman he had known before he came to the Lord. When he saw her again, he felt the Lord told him he would marry her. He kept quiet about it. Then many months later, after the woman had become discipled and grounded in the Word through our ministry, he courted her. They married and have built a truly remarkable marriage together. Bob's business has also prospered and the newlyweds have bought a house. Today Bob is a minister helping with pastoral care, while running a full-time business to support his "real" work.

HE WILL COME TO WHERE WE GO

Jesus made a great promise to the disciples. As He commissioned them to go out two by two, He promised that if they would go, He would go with them to every city and place He sent them (see Luke 10:1).

God is about to move like we have never seen before. But we must be faithful to go where He sends us. Are we willing to make the sacrifices? Will we be laborers to help in the mighty harvest of souls? Are we willing to work with believers of different ethnic groups or different denominations to reach our cities? Will we say yes to whatever it takes?

The Lord wants to send you and me ahead of Him tc the way for His coming. Wherever we set our feet to go, His tan gible presence will be there. Whether we go into the neighbor- hood streets or to a foreign field, the result will be the same: If we are faithful to go where He leads, He will show up in a pow- erful way.

If we are going to reach this generation, we must do more than just get together for fellowship and prayer. Yes, prayer is foundational, but we must pray with purpose. Fasting helps us die to our flesh, but we must fast with purpose.

The prophet Isaiah clarified the purpose for times of prayer and fasting. We are told that if we "loose the chains of injustice" by reaching out and providing help to those who cannot break free from their circumstances, then our healing will come quick- ly (see Isa. 58:8).

Are you ready to move from passive prayer and fasting (v. 5) to justice in action? (vv. 6-10).

Note

1. *Christian History,* vol. 19, Issue 65, 2000, pp. 36, 37.

CHAPTER SEVEN

Be in pain, and labor to bring forth, O daughter of Zion,
like a woman in birth pangs.

MICAH 4:10

P.U.S.H.
(PRAY UNTIL SOMETHING HAPPENS!)

Randy's overbearing, abusive father wounded him deeply as a child. Spankings always turned into beatings. Irritation usually turned into rage. At a young age, Randy would retreat to his bedroom to escape reality by exercising his artistic imagination in dance. During his teens, his dance abilities became a form of identity and a way to receive affirmation. He won championships and soon earned a name for himself as a rising star.

By his early 20s, Randy's dance troupe "The Love Machine" was an opening act for major concerts and he worked for radio stations and nightclubs. But the life of professional dancing was a nightmare for him. Inside the studio, dancers forced their bodies to perform; but outside they destroyed their bodies with eating disorders, drug addictions and dangerous sexual relationships. Addicted to the accolades brought on by performance, Randy lived from show to show, waiting for the next applause, waiting to be "discovered" and living between shows in misery. Randy could never outrun the horrid feelings left over from the sick relationship he had experienced with his father.

Randy came to my old fitness studio and offered to swap aerobics instruction for studio time to rehearse his dance troupe. I had just prayed my agonizing prayer in the back room to make myself available to God, and I welcomed Randy wholeheartedly. One of the first evenings he was there, he came to church with me and gave his heart to the Lord, and immediately took to the streets with me to witness.

Although at the time it was a bizarre concept to dance inside a church building, as God reconstructed Randy in spirit, soul and body, he had a growing idea that he might be able to use his gift of dance to help further the Kingdom. Randy ministered where he was but prayed in earnest for the chance to dance for the Lord. Like Henry Ford who built a car, and then had to build roads on which to drive them, Randy now had to pray for churches in which he could exercise his gift. Randy *prayed*.

As we walked the streets, worked out physically and lived by faith financially, prayer proved to be more valuable a lesson than anything else we ever learned. We didn't know what to do when demon-possessed people lunged at us or when we found out we'd brought home someone who had just overdosed, but we did learn how to pray. We didn't know how we'd pay the bills or feed the hungry people all around us, but we learned how to pray until something happened.

In 1997, Edwin Louis Cole spoke at Prayer Mountain. He saw a banner we'd hung that read P.U.S.H. (Pray Until Something Happens) and commented, "That sounds like a woman in labor." I thought about it for a moment and realized that's exactly what it meant! God wants to birth something through us.

Any woman who has experienced childbirth understands the perseverance and strength required. Most women would say the pain is excruciating. But as intense as the labor pains are, great joy comes with the first glimpse of the child. Words cannot describe the love, thankfulness and peace experienced by a mother and father after a safe delivery.

LIKE A WOMAN TRAVAILING IN LABOR, WE MUST PRAY THROUGH THE BIRTHING PROCESS FOR SOULS WHO HAVE NOT YET RESPONDED TO THE GOSPEL.

The process is no different when laboring for God's kingdom. The pain is intense, the hours of labor are often long, but oh, the joy that comes with each soul's birth into the Kingdom!

I once heard an evangelist say, "With one ear we listen to the sweet melodies of heaven, and with the other ear we hear the cries of hell." We live inside an intense battle raging over people's souls. The Spirit of the Lord is upon us to preach good news, liberty and healing, and we have been commissioned by the Lord to share this message (see Isa. 61:1,2). Like a woman travailing in labor, we must pray through the birthing process for the souls who have not yet responded to the gospel.

God alone knows what it will take to turn a heart toward Him. He gives us the privilege to pray with perseverance for someone's soul. Even when things don't seem to be happening, we must look on the situation with eyes of faith and not gaze on the natural circumstances. We must trust the Lord's wisdom, because He alone knows the things He is working out in someone's life.

Burning up the Dross

Many Christians today are praying for a move of God that will impact thousands of souls, but if we believe God is going to move, we have to prepare our own hearts. We must examine our own lives and allow Him to show us the things in us that are displeasing to Him.

Who are we when no one else is looking? It is what we do behind closed doors, where no one else can see us, that determines the power of God or lack of it in public. We must be the same people in our prayer closets as we are in public prayer meetings.

In times at the altar, many of us pray for God's holy fire to consume us, but I am not sure we know what we're asking for. Have the flames become so intense that the only thing left burning within us is holy hunger for Him? Has the fire of God ignited a burning passion within us for His purposes? That is the Lord's desire. As we examine what those revival flames actually do, our lives will be changed and our prayers will ascend to God as a sweet aroma.

God is going to burn out the dross in our lives, and He is going to shake all that can be shaken. Hebrews 12 addresses this type of shaking and goes on to tell us to offer to God acceptable worship, with reverence and awe "for our God is a consuming fire" (Heb. 12:29). Acceptable worship to the Lord requires a heart that honors Him.

Simple obedience is one of the highest forms of worship. God is looking for people who have an obedient, sacrificial servant's heart. We must walk with humility and a fear of the Lord. Only that is acceptable worship and is pleasing in His sight. Once our hearts are broken before Him, He can consume us with His flames and make us catalysts for revival in others.

PRAYING THROUGH FOR BREAKTHROUGH

For a time, Randy struggled to leave behind his old reasons for dance to become pure in heart and gain his acceptance and approval from the applause of heaven, not from man. He struggled with overcoming the bitterness toward his father that slumbered in an easy chair in his heart. As he prayed, he pushed, and things began to happen. First, Randy became a new creation in Christ. Then churches started changing their ways to embrace the idea of dance in ministry, and doors began to fly open to him. When the breakthrough came, Randy's heart was ready. He has now danced all over the world and is recognized internationally as one of the pioneers of modern Christian dance. Even more exciting, Randy has won many people to Christ.

To see spiritual breakthroughs we have to keep asking until the answer comes; we have to keep knocking until the doors open. Laboring to bring forth revival, whether personal or corporate, is no easy process. We cannot make God move, but the condition of our hearts tells Him if we are ready for Him to move. We must travail and persevere like a woman during an intense labor before birthing a baby. Too often we want God to move His hand for revival; but if we would touch His heart, He would naturally move His hand.

The apostle Paul exemplified tenacity and perseverance: "I press toward the goal for the prize of the upward call of God in Christ Jesus" (Phil. 3:14). Notice that there is a process of pressing in, of enduring to run the race to completion. Our bodies get fatigued, and our minds battle thoughts like, *I can't do it. It's too hard; it's too long; there's no way I can make it.* But the Spirit says, "You can do it. Because of what Christ has already done, you can go the distance." Jesus has already run the race, and He is the joy set before us.

How do we persevere when our minds battle the thought that we are doomed to fail? We push forward anyway. We call on a fellow Christian and ask for prayer. We saturate our minds in the Word because we are promised that "[God] will keep him in perfect peace, whose mind is stayed on You" (Isa. 26:3). We renew our minds by washing them in the water of the Word. We hold on to Him at all cost.

Our minds are the gateway to our hearts. If we give our minds to the things of this world, then eventually the world will have our hearts as well. If we focus on the Lord, then He remains in the center of our minds and hearts. We must commit ourselves to persist until we have finished the race in righteousness, bringing honor to Him.

THE PRICE OF REVIVAL

Storms are certain to come; how we weather them is determined by the focus of our hearts. May the Lord be able to say of us, as He did of the Church of Philadelphia, "I know your works. See,

I have set before you an open door, and no one can shut it; for you have a little strength, have kept My word, and have not denied My name" (Rev. 3:8). The Lord is giving us open doors for the gospel. Though we may feel we have but a little strength, we need to keep running through those doors. We need to press in and pray for more changed lives and more souls to come to Christ.

We may think we have little to offer, but whatever we offer back to the Lord in purity of heart will be sufficient for what He asks us to do. We can choose to press in or we can faint along the way. God is strengthening you and me right now to press in just a little more and a little longer. If we submit to the Lord and ask Him to build His character in us, then victory is on the way.

Are we willing to pay the price for revival? Do things in our lives and attitudes of our hearts hinder a move of God? Revivals of the past have always begun with a deep hunger for intimacy with God. From that place of intimacy comes repentance, consecration and holiness.

Let's keep our focus on Jesus—on worshiping Him. Even though we sometimes see spectacular manifestations of His Spirit, the greatest miracles are revealed in changed lives.

*Jesus came and spoke to them, saying, "All authority has been given to Me
in heaven and on earth. Go therefore and make disciples of all the nations,
baptizing them in the name of the Father and of the Son and of the Holy Spirit,
teaching them to observe all things that I have commanded you; and lo, I am
with you always, even to the end of the age." Amen.*
MATTHEW 28:18-20

WATER THE
CAMELS

Years ago, near Christmas time, I was driving to a Luv Ya
Houston men's meeting hosted by E. Z. Jones. Near the onramp
of the freeway there was a man holding a sign that read "Corpus
Christi." He had a suitcase with him. I was running late that day
and, unwilling to make myself even later, I started to pass him
when I felt a tug to stop. I called to him, saying, "Have you eaten
lunch?" When he said no, I invited him to come with me and tell
me what was going on with him. I learned that he was a com-
puter programmer who had lost his job in Michigan. There was
a possible job opportunity for him in Corpus Christ.

I carried his suitcase into the restaurant and into the lunch meeting. When all the businessmen who had passed him by on their way to lunch saw him, conviction fell. As a result, the compassion of God touched everyone there and E.Z. Jones felt led to take up an offering for this man.

After the lunch, I took him into my apartment for a short period of time to get him through Christmas. During that time he became a Christian. After a few weeks he felt led to return to Michigan, where I heard later that he became involved in a church and also got back into business.

One particular businessman who attended that Luv Ya Houston meeting was in the oil business. He had been invited numerous times before, but this was the first time he had attended. Years later he was on television and told the story of what caused him to become a Christian. The final event that brought him to the Lord was seeing a man carrying a suitcase into a restaurant and another man following him, where an offering was taken up to help the stranger. That day he saw the love of Christians and the compassion of Jesus poured out through a group of businessmen and was propelled toward Christ.

PREPARING OUR HEARTS

People are crying out to God for revival in their own lives and for their families, their cities and their nation. Yet this only comes with a price. God is looking for a people—a Bride—with a prepared heart into which He can deposit His rich authority. The Bride who will usher this generation into a relationship with the Lord must be willing to serve and to sacrifice.

The late revivalist Leonard Ravenhill once reminded my staff, "When a sacrifice is placed on the altar, the fire does not consume the altar but the sacrifice on the altar." We are that sacrifice placed on God's altar as we daily offer ourselves to Him and make ourselves available for His purposes.

Hearts that are prepared to serve and sacrifice are also willing to receive the needy people He brings our way. Some have been battered by the consequences of sin, and they may not look like the kind of people we want to hang out with. Yet if we are willing to serve them for the Lord's sake, God promises to give us power and authority to be His witnesses.

More and more frequently, Christians are gathering in humility and asking, "God, what is Your will for the Body of Christ in our city?" Together we are becoming a corporate, anointed people who say, "God, not our will, but Your will be done." We are becoming servants who make sacrifices for souls as we serve, individually and as a body of believers, this generation of people who so desperately need the Lord.

TAMING THE TENSIONS

One of the gaps in our society is generational. Often we have allowed that gap to hinder us from reaching out to young people. Generation gaps have caused seemingly impenetrable walls of misunderstanding between parent and child. The mistrust is even more evident among youth from broken homes.

Gang violence is on the rise as many youth turn to gangs as substitute families. Gangs provide an identity and a group—a place to belong. Are we, the Body of Christ, sharing Christ's love in a way that reflects a sense of family that would draw such teens in? As violence escalates and spreads from our inner cities to suburbia and even into small town environments, our ministry of reconciliation means that we are the true peacemakers in a troubled world.

When I approached my second decade of ministry, I wondered if young people would still relate to what I shared with them. Yet the Lord continued and still continues to lead our team to the young. Some people in our ministry can identify with them; others come from quite different backgrounds. Regardless, when we reach out to young people with the love of Christ, they embrace it.

One day, one of our workers, Bob, joined me for a time of ministry at a home for troubled teens. Bob noticed how hardened and angry many of the teens were and asked them why. One young man replied, "Don't you know? We're Generation X. Our parents didn't care. We're not supposed to care."

The kids initially didn't want to talk with us because of their feelings of bitterness. They weren't angry with us, they were responding to their own hurting hearts. Eventually the ice was broken, and we began to relate to them at their point of need. I said, "You know, some people really don't care, but there's Somebody who does care. He cares so much that He gave His own life for you." As uncomfortable as it might be to reach out to angry young people, we take the first step, and God takes it from there.

On the Cutting Edge

Society has called today's young generation Gen-Xers, but I refer to them as Gen-Edgers, or teen-edgers—young people living on the edge of eternity. As we sow our time and our wisdom into them and they get saved, they move to the cutting edge for Christ. Like Joshua and Caleb, they see things differently from others who spy out the Promised Land. We must dedicate ourselves to releasing these young people to their destiny, for we desperately need their vision to lead us into the revival God has for us. Without their youthful vision, we will all perish in the wilderness of endless wandering.

WE MUST DEDICATE OURSELVES TO RELEASING YOUNG PEOPLE TO THEIR DESTINY, FOR WE DESPERATELY NEED THEIR VISION TO LEAD US INTO THE REVIVAL GOD HAS FOR US.

This generation is radical and unashamed of the gospel. As I watch our young people working in the harvest or singing passionately in the choir, I can't help but say to myself, *There's my girl! That's my boy!* There is no greater joy in life than having spiritual sons and daughters whom the Lord has redeemed.

Many of our youth, however, are wandering aimlessly and without hope, bearing the derogatory name Generation X, when God wants them to become a generation of excellence. As you and I fulfill our calling to serve them, they will fulfill their God-given potential and do mighty exploits for the gospel.

Hundreds of years before Christ's birth, the prophet Malachi spoke of these days in which we live: "Behold, I will send you Elijah the prophet before the coming of the great and dreadful day of the LORD. And he will turn the hearts of the fathers to the children, and the hearts of the children to their fathers" (Mal. 4:5,6). God wants to use you and me to reach this fatherless, orphaned generation.

Many on-fire Christian youth are ministering to others, and God is also using fathers in the faith and spiritual mothers to reach young hearts. With so many growing up without a dad, it is beautiful to see men of God embrace these hard-to-reach young people.

Take, for example, Pastor Mike Huss of West Oaks Community Church in Alief, a suburb of Southwest Houston. This church linked up with Somebody Cares Houston and became involved in the Adopt-a-Gang prayer coverage. Mike's church adopted several gangs in the Alief area to pray for them. Then the church moved from intercession to intervention, and the youth responded. What began as a youth-oriented Friday evening service with about 20 attending has grown to a Saturday evening church comprised of 250 to 300 young people of various racial and cultural backgrounds, including many kids from gangs. Now the church is reaching out to their families, and lives are being changed. It all started with a burden to pray for young people.

Bud Lenz, former staff member, and now missionary with his family in Peru, and Richard Hinojosa, who worked at the citywide baptism at the water park, were part of an initial group of youth ministers who developed an arm of Somebody Cares known as Youth Guidance Consultants (YGC). YGC has provided training to volunteers, teachers, school officials and community service workers who work with at-risk youth and gang members. The hands-on work with the youth started as Richard reached out to young people in a local public school. He simply hung out with the kids during lunchtime and built relationships with them and with their teachers and principals.

Eventually, with Richard's help, we developed a six-hour training seminar to identify and intervene in cases of at-risk youth behavior, which helped teachers and administrators deal with real-life questions, such as how to break up a fight. Working together with Ernie Lopez, Max Torres and Bud Lenz, we then developed a handbook that is so effective it has been used by school districts and the Houston mayor's Anti-Gang Task Force. The Houston police department outreach division adopted it as a training manual. Those of our group who completed it received I.D. badges provided by the police department to go work in schools.

Richard Hinojosa also developed the "Hero" curriculum, a biblically based character-development curriculum that is now being used in secular schools. Community leaders are taking notice of the program's effectiveness, and they want to know more about it.

Restoring Hearts in a Fatherless Society

Today God is calling the Church to go forth in the spirit of an Elijah or a John the Baptist to prepare this generation for His coming. As preparation is made for the Lord's return, many in this generation will have hearts turned back not only to their earthly fathers but also to the heavenly Father.

A few years ago, a 14-year-old boy on the streets told us, "Mom had to choose between me and her boyfriend—and I lost." Over the years we have worked with many runaways and teen prostitutes. One of these young women said that she was left at a motel to fend for herself at the age of eight. To reach this generation of young people, we need to understand this breakdown of the parental role. I am particularly sensitive to this problem, for I often felt unsettled following my own parents' divorce when I was a young boy.

Our cities are filled with young people who are virtual orphans—victims of an increasingly fatherless society. Can you feel the pain and hopelessness of this fatherless generation? Do you see why they feel destined for destruction instead of success? As one kid on the street told me, "There are only two ways off the streets—the penitentiary or the grave." Fortunately, Jesus offers a real alternative.

Passing the Baton to a Radical Generation

"Generation Jesus" in Houston is having a great impact on the next generation. They are a devoted group of young people ranging in age from teens to late 20s. Many of them have lived radical lives of sin but now have turned their hearts toward Christ. They are led by E. Z. Jones, the man who gave me an apartment to live in almost two decades ago.

E. Z. and Lena Jones could choose to be uninvolved with young people by using the excuse that they're from another era; or they could cast judgmental stares at the green-haired, body-pierced young people around them. Instead, they are pastors to this on-fire group of young people. Teens often knock on their door at one or two o'clock in the morning, but E. Z. and Lena would rather be awakened in the middle of the night than identify their young people in the morgue or officiate at their funerals.

Former addicts and gang leaders are so hungry for God that when it's time for the weekly Generation Jesus services to end, they don't want to leave. These teens are growing quickly as disciples of the Lord. As E. Z. says, "They don't ask each other 'What church do you go to?' They just love each other, pray with each other and praise God together."

One day, E. Z. called me following a powerful night of ministry with Generation Jesus. He said, "I looked around the room, reflected on what the Lord was doing, and suddenly realized this is the clubhouse of the same apartment complex where you had a move of God in the 1980s! I looked out the clubhouse window and saw the apartment we rented for you, Doug."

E. Z. reminisced about the time he walked into my apartment and saw a bunch of young people sleeping on the floor. In the same clubhouse where Generation Jesus first held its meetings, I held Bible studies with those young people. E. Z. and Lena asked if I would come one evening and minister to Generation Jesus, pray for the young people and symbolically pass the baton. My heart rejoiced that from a seed planted years ago a new breed of radical youth has arisen to reach their generation for Christ.

While some may have given up hope for the coming generation, God certainly has not. Many young people are finding direction and purpose for their lives. There is a rising hunger among the youth. God is giving them a mantle of John the Baptist. They have a prophetic mantle to stand and declare, "Prepare ye the way of the Lord" to their generation.

Today many young people are being reached and are ministering to others with fervor and zeal. We have a responsibility to encourage them and share with them any wisdom we may have gleaned during our years in ministry.

In Search of the Bride

Abraham once sent out a servant in search of a bride for his son, Isaac (see Gen. 24). Likewise, our heavenly Father is sending out His Holy Spirit to search for a Bride for His Son, Jesus. Throughout Scripture we find types and shadows, people and events that represent a message the Lord is sharing with us today. In this Genesis passage, Abraham represents a type of the heavenly Father, and his servant represents a type of the Holy Spirit. Isaac is a type of Jesus, and the bride represents the Church.

When Abraham sent out his servant, he gave him 10 camels. These camels carried the basic necessities for traveling through the desert and bore gifts to bestow upon the bride. Today the heavenly Father has sent out His Holy Spirit in search of a Bride prepared to serve Him and people in need. As we, the Church, become that Bride for Jesus, the heavenly Father bestows upon us His provision and His gifts.

The key trait Abraham's servant sought in a bride for Isaac was that she be willing to serve her master and those in need. Abraham's servant stopped at the town well and found such a woman. She gave him a drink of water and was also willing to water his 10 thirsty camels, which were also dirty, hungry and stinky.

I have heard it said that one camel having completed that desert journey could drink approximately 40 gallons of water. Ten camels would then need 400 gallons of water, and this young woman drew it all from the well! As she served those camels, she did not realize that on their backs they were bearing gifts she would receive. She looked not for the gifts but simply for the opportunity to serve. In the same way, the heavenly Father is looking for a Bride for His Son—a Bride who is willing to serve Him and those thirsty camels.

Many of us are like those dirty, stinky, thirsty camels coming out of the wilderness. We have pasts filled with addictive behaviors, immoral lifestyles and futile searches to satisfy our longing souls. But God has fed us and cleaned us up.

This current generation has the same needs. They are trying countless ways to cover up their fears, insecurities and pain. God wants to transform them into a John-the-Baptist generation, preparing the way of the Lord. As their lives are changed through Christ, this generation of young people will be true witnesses who rescue others.

SERVING AND SAVING THIS GENERATION

The prophet Joel recorded: "It shall come to pass afterward that I will pour out My Spirit on all flesh; your sons and your daughters shall prophesy, your old men shall dream dreams, your young men shall see visions. And also on My menservants and on My maidservants I will pour out My Spirit in those days" (Joel 2:28,29).

Genuine prophets and prophetesses are those who will live a radical life for God and boldly proclaim His truth and mercy to a generation coming out of the desert. Today's young people are keenly aware of where they have been and the heartache they have experienced. As they come to know the living God, they become radical for God. They are not ashamed of the gospel of Christ, for they have experienced it as the power of God for salvation (see Rom. 1:16). Because they have wandered in the wilderness of life, today's young people are destined to become a prophetic generation, proclaiming the word of the Lord and preparing the way for His coming.

God loves the coming generation and wants to set them free. He is giving you and me the opportunity and the privilege to boldly share the gospel with them. But are we willing to work with those whom we might consider to be unlovely? Will we go the extra mile with them? God is challenging us to get out of our comfort zone and reach out to others with a servant's heart and sacrificial love.

Now it shall come to pass in the latter days that the mountain of the LORD's house shall be established on the top of the mountains, and shall be exalted above the hills; and all nations shall flow to it. Many people shall come and say, "Come, and let us go up to the mountain of the LORD, to the house of the God of Jacob; He will teach us His ways, and we shall walk in His paths."
For out of Zion shall go forth the law, and the word of the LORD from Jerusalem. He shall judge between the nations, and rebuke many people; they shall beat their swords into plowshares, and their spears into pruning hooks; nation shall not lift up sword against nation, neither shall they learn war anymore."

ISAIAH 2:2-4 (CF. MICAH 4:1-3)

REVIVAL BY CHOICE OR BY JUDGMENT?

Some years ago, God moved my heart to start a regular Sunday service for those saved through our ministry. For years I resisted the idea, even when those same people told me they felt awkward going immediately to mainline churches and needed a transition place to gather. I believed I was called to build the Body of Christ in the city and identify and encourage the ministries already established rather than start a local church myself. But when pastors started urging me as well, I prayed earnestly, then rented a hotel room as a meeting place.

First we called the new church Edge City, then changed the name to Turning Point Christian Center. We opened the membership to those who came to Jesus through our ministry and to those who came with a letter of release and blessing from their local pastor. If a Christian wanted to join us, we told the person that he or she could come as a missionary under the auspices of a local church and return to that local church when the mission was accomplished.

I disbanded the church once, telling the members their transition period was over and they needed to get attached to local churches. Two months later I reopened the doors and started again, and we immediately grew with new converts and those who had not been able to become involved elsewhere.

Over time, a more permanent office and meeting facility was established. The ministry and church continue to grow as those who come have a heart for reaching the lost.

This unusual approach is not God's pattern for most churches. But because we focus on service and sacrifice, our membership knows without a doubt that our goal is to help pastor a whole city, and we will do whatever it takes to see the citywide united Body of Christ meet the needs of our community.

We have to be willing to do whatever God asks in order to see more of His purposes come to pass in our cities. In my heart I know there is more—more unity to be nurtured, more perseverance needed, more brokenness and more souls to be added. I teach our converts that true revival will first be a revival of holiness and consecration.

I often pray, "Lord, how are You going to set Your Church ablaze with a hunger for Your holiness?" We say we want revival and we want the Church to work together to be part of a harvest. Yet at times our actions speak a contrary message. What will it take to bring a lasting revival to our land? There is nothing wrong with going to services and having the Lord minister to us in a way that makes us feel good, but there is more to revival than that. In fact, there are times when our need is not for something to make us feel good. Before there can be genuine times of refreshing, there must be times of repentance.

Have we been broken before the Lord over our own sin, including sins of omission? Our sin doesn't have to be something we've done; sometimes it is something we have left undone. We must ask ourselves whether we are truly concerned for the welfare of others. A move of God that does not lead to changed lives and lost souls coming to Christ falls short of being a true revival. A genuine revival is not a matter of hoopla or emotion or even spiritual refreshing; it is a matter of transforming individuals and then entire communities.

AT A CROSSROADS

A few years ago on a radio program, I was asked if I thought God was going to bring judgment or revival to America. I paused for a moment and replied, "Both." God is going to bring revival to His people, and it will either come by choice or by judgment. We are at a crossroads as a nation and as the Church. The choices we make today will determine our future.

The late Dr. Richard Halverson, chaplain of the U.S. Senate from 1981 to 1994, and author of several books, succinctly summed up the history of the Church: "Christianity started in Palestine as a relationship with a person—Jesus. It went to Greece

and became a philosophy, went to Rome and became an
tion, and went to Europe and became a culture. Then it can.
America and became an enterprise."

The Lord will not force us to consecrate our lives, but He can
surely put pressure on us to seek Him. He will do whatever it
takes to get our attention. We will either surrender all to Him
and birth revival or, through our disobedience, He will allow
judgment to come. We will go to our knees to seek Him either by
choice or by judgment.

If we do not rise up and fulfill our calling to prepare people
for His coming, God will have to shake us. Therefore, we must
lay aside anything that hinders us, individually or corporately.
We cannot give in to fears and insecurities or engage in blame.
This is not a time to play games with God. His Word states that
everything that can be shaken will be shaken until only that
which cannot be shaken remains (see Heb. 12:26,27).

Although it is never God's desire to bring destruction, He
wants our total devotion. He desires to possess the thrones of
our hearts. When the Lord breathes His life in us and through
us, nothing can stop His impact on our lives and communities.
How will we withstand the wind and the shaking? It all depends
on the condition of our hearts.

HANG ON!

Three things will take place during shaking. For one, those who
have left their first-love relationship with the Lord will be shak-
en until they return to God's stern but merciful, loving hand.

Obstacles in the way of the gospel will also be removed, such
as people or ministries that are cosmetic only. Jesus told a parable about a landowner who came seeking fruit on his fig tree but
found none. From a distance, the fig tree probably had plenty of

leaves and must have appeared capable of bearing figs. But as the owner approached, he was disappointed that no figs were to be found (see Luke 13:6-9). If those who produce only leaves but no fruit refuse to repent, God will replace them with those who are preaching the pure gospel and bearing genuine fruit.

During the shaking God will also restore those who feel forsaken—those who have served the Lord with sincerity and integrity, fighting the good fight and loving the sheep, yet have become weary of well doing (see Gal. 6:9). Those who have been faithful through all the trials and have kept their stand for God's righteousness will receive blessings in order to perpetuate the gospel and experience a great outpouring of God's Spirit.

GOD IS LOOKING FOR A PEOPLE WHO ARE HUNGRY FOR HIS CHARACTER AND A DEEPER RELATIONSHIP WITH HIM—A PEOPLE WHO PURSUE HOLINESS OVER HAPPINESS.

Beyond the shaking is the promise and the hope set before us. We must pray for our ministers and leaders as they undergo relentless attacks during shaking, and for the Body of Christ as well. This is not a day to give up on the Church, or yourself, and certainly not on the Lord. Instead, it is a day for us to get on our knees and seek the Lord for His grace.

He is raising up people who want to see a true outpouring of the Holy Spirit. It will not be limited to any one crusade or meet-

ing, but the Holy Spirit will move through individuals, ministries
and churches that are prepared. God is looking for a people who
are hungry for His character and a deeper relationship with Him—
a people who pursue holiness over happiness. He will shake anything in our lives that distracts us from Him, so we must seek Him
with all our hearts and press in to Him as never before.

THE LATTER RAIN IS STARTING

Bob Ferguson, wearing one of his ever-present baseball caps,
walked alone into a Friday Night Alive meeting, looking like a
stereotypical Houston redneck and not at all like the recovering
heroin addict he really was. Bob's father had died, leaving Bob
feeling empty inside. When his AA sponsor died as well, Bob's
heart quit feeling anything except a steady ache.

When people from AA dropped out of the group occasionally to attend church, Bob would become angry. "They think
they're too good for us," he reasoned. Finally, when another
friend became a Christian, Bob asked, "What are you doing?"

"Man, I'm getting to know Jesus!" the friend said.

Bob had grown up in a traditional church and believed in
the one true God, but he had never learned about Jesus. The concept intrigued him. One night, during an eight-week series at
Friday Night Alive, Bob gave his life to the Lord. While I was
teaching on "The Work of the Cross," he came forward, saying,
"God is real! God is real!" and started weeping.

"Man, You're slick," Bob told God as he confessed Christ as
His Lord. Suddenly he knew that Jesus was the way to the Father
and that he was no longer alone. He realized that no matter who
came or went on earth, he would never be fatherless again.

Each week Bob continued to weep as he listened with a
grateful heart. He knew he was finally hearing unvarnished,

absolute truth. A month later he asked about baptism, and we baptized him that night in the hot tub at the Holiday Inn.

Bob was exuberant in his Christian witness. I had been teaching on the spirit of adoption that we receive through Christ, and Bob found everyone he could to adopt. He took literally the idea that he was now a minister of reconciliation, regardless of the lack of certificates hanging on his wall. Weeks later, on a campout with a friend, Bob took out his Bible for morning devotions.

"You going thumping?" his friend chided, thinking Bob was going to start preaching.

"I'm having my morning prayer," Bob replied. "Want to be included?"

Scriptures popped into Bob's mind and he shared them with his friend, and the man repented and received Christ. Then the friend asked Bob to baptize him right there in the lake. Bob didn't know what to do except just to do it, so he baptized his friend in the name of the Father, the Son and the Holy Spirit.

"I'm 99.5 percent certain that you're okay, but you'd better get baptized again when we get back, just in case," Bob told the man. Immediately he remembered that Jesus had called him to minister and he said, "I take it back. You're 100 percent legal. You're baptized, man!"

LETTING OUR LIGHT SHINE

Isaiah wrote, "Arise, shine; for your light has come!" (Isa. 60:1). Though we know the light of the Lord is going to get brighter, the following verse reads, "Darkness shall cover the earth." As God's light gets brighter, darkness will get darker, yet God will pour out great wonders. "I will show wonders in the heavens and in the earth: blood and fire and pillars of smoke. The sun shall be turned into darkness, and the moon into blood, before the coming of the great and terrible day of the LORD" (Joel 2:30,31).

As God pours out His Spirit, we are also going to see an onslaught of the enemy. We must prepare, let go of old ways and become lovers of truth, so we will not be deceived by the schemes and temptations of the evil one.

Scripture warns of false prophets in the last days and predicts that many people will reject the truth because they want their ears tickled—they want to hear only what makes them feel good. No matter how uncomfortable the truth makes us feel, we must love it more than life itself, for it is the truth that sets us free (see John 8:32).

We also need to be planted in the household of faith when the dark gets darker. We are instructed in Scripture not to forsake the fellowship of the saints, and this will be all the more crucial in the days preceding the return of Christ (see Heb. 10:25). We must care for one another, helping our brothers and sisters in their maturing process as believers. Likewise, we must prepare to take in those who will find shelter under the wings of God.

The prophet Joel said, "It shall come to pass that whoever calls on the name of the LORD shall be saved" (Joel 2:32). Peter quotes this verse, as does Paul (see Acts 2:21; Rom. 10:13). Joel continues, "For in Mount Zion and in Jerusalem there shall be deliverance." Deliverance can only come as an outcome of the salvation of the Lord. God wants to bring salvation, healing and deliverance to our lives and to the lives of those He will redeem during this great outpouring.

We cannot separate the terms "salvation" and "deliverance," for with salvation comes deliverance. That is the hope for our lives and for the multitudes still in the valley of decision. The Lord is calling people to Himself.

Bob Ferguson is a great example of this kind of outpouring. His love for God is so exuberant, so irrepressible, that dozens and perhaps hundreds of people by now have followed him into salvation. He's just a regular guy, a former heroin junkie, who loves and exudes truth wherever he goes.

Between the Porch and the Altar

We love to hear about revival happening to others, but we also long to see a mighty outpouring of God's Spirit in our own lives, as on the day of Pentecost. Scripture says: "Let the priests, who minister to the LORD, weep between the porch and the altar" (Joel 2:17). Who are the priests referred to here? That's us, because we are a royal priesthood, a holy nation (see 1 Pet. 2:9). We must repent and weep between the porch and the altar. We must stand between the living and the dead and stop the plague of sin (see Num. 16:48). How is the plague stopped? By personal repentance and revival, which brings personal refreshing. At that place of brokenness in *our* lives, the plague of sin will be stopped in *their* lives.

Any of us who are or want to be considered leaders must weep between the porch and the altar. The apostle Paul said, "Imitate me, just as I imitate Christ" (see 1 Cor. 11:1). We must set an example that Jesus would want the sheep to follow. Joel issued a charge to ministers to cry out to the Lord, saying, "Spare Your people, O LORD, and do not give Your heritage to reproach, that the nations should rule over them. Why should they say among the peoples, 'Where is their God?'" (Joel 2:17).

The world is desperate to see that what Christians have is the real deal. As tragedies are reported on the nightly news all over the world, people are awaiting the Church's response. Faced with fires, riots, murders, economic crashes and more, people wonder, *Where is God?* We must show them by manifesting His glory and power in the midst of tragedy.

I believe we are living on borrowed time. Those who are producing fruit will be pruned so they will produce even more or better fruit. Those who are not producing fruit will be moved aside to make room for those who will. God will show us both His goodness and His severity (see Rom. 11:22). It begins with

THE WORLD IS DESPERATE TO SEE THAT WHAT CHRISTIANS HAVE IS THE REAL DEAL.

us. In other words, those outside the Church must see the love and power of God in action through living, breathing temples of the Holy Spirit—that's you and me. *Our preaching will have more impact when our message is something we actually live.* When we go forth as witnesses for Christ, walking in the love of God, then God will begin to manifest His presence, and signs, wonders and miracles will follow.

MAKING WAY FOR THE NEW

The Lord said, through the prophet Joel, "Behold, I will send you grain and new wine and oil" (Joel 2:19). A grain has to die so that new grain can spring up (see John 12:24). For our vats to be full of new wine and oil, the old has to be emptied out. We have to let go of the old nature, the old ways, to have the new things God has in store for us. We must let go even of the good so we can have that which is better.

When God begins to pour out His Spirit upon us, often He begins to shake up our lives so that the things that can be shaken fall down and the things that cannot be shaken are left standing. God begins to fill us with a new perception of things, a new way of thinking, a new attitude, a new character.

When that process is complete, He is able to pour out His Spirit because He can trust us to be vessels He can fill with His power.

God took the children of Israel out of Egypt, but before they could enter the Promised Land He had to *take Egypt out of them*. When we go through the wilderness experiences of life, God deals with the sins of Egypt that still reside in our hearts.

When we seek God's face and cry out to Him for personal revival, He will begin to reveal our false beliefs, areas of disobedience and bad attitudes. He removes old ways and teaches us His ways. He uproots the remnants of the old nature and shows us the things that need to die. As we trust Him to do this work, transformation begins. We become ready for the new grain, the new wine and the new oil.

God has been transforming us into His image since the day we accepted Christ. He wants the old nature crucified so that we can fulfill His purposes upon the earth. Paul encourages us, "Therefore, if anyone is in Christ, he is a new creation; old things have passed away; behold, all things have become new" (2 Cor. 5:17). When we come to the cross of Christ, we come to a place of death—death to self. Our old nature is buried so we can rise up in newness to an abundant life in Christ. But to receive the newness God desires for us, we have to die to the past.

Old wheat has to die; old wineskins have to go. Old oil in the chalice must be poured out so He can fill it with new oil. "Behold all things have become new" is God's desire. We cannot bypass the death process. The apostle Paul said, "Therefore put to death your members which are on the earth: fornication, uncleanness, passion, evil desire, and covetousness, which is idolatry" (Col. 3:5). Why should we put such things to death? Because holding

on to them means denying Christ's lordship in those
our lives.

Paul goes on to warn that "the wrath of God is coming upon
the sons of disobedience" (Col. 3:6). Let's not be found to be dis-
obedient children, even though we might have been in the past.
And let us not merely settle for external or cosmetic righteousness, for Paul continues: "But now you yourselves are to put off
all these: anger, wrath, malice, blasphemy, filthy language out of
your mouth" (Col. 3:8). After dealing with overt sins in the previous verses, Paul emphasizes that God also wants to deal with
anger and other matters of the heart.

All Things Become New

In the death and renewal process, first the outward sins are
cleansed and then He begins to deal with us about matters of the
heart—our thoughts, attitudes and words. We are in a spiritual
battle, but it is not only against satanic principalities and pow-
ers. The battle begins in our minds:

> For though we walk in the flesh, we do not war accord-
> ing to the flesh. For the weapons of our warfare are not
> carnal but mighty in God for pulling down strongholds,
> casting down arguments and every high thing that exalts
> itself against the knowledge of God, bringing every
> thought into captivity to the obedience of Christ, and
> being ready to punish all disobedience when your obedi-
> ence is fulfilled (2 Cor. 10:3-6).

God wants to take us to an intimate place of relationship
with Him. He wants to show us His manifest presence and glory.
He wants to show us great and awesome things and use us to

reach our generation. Will we become vessels into which He can pour His Spirit? Will we be vessels of honor into which He can deposit His power for His purpose?

JESUS DID IT

Almost everyone from our new converts congregation is involved in some form of ministry somewhere in our city. Bob Ferguson, the least likely to have become a true minister, is ablaze with the fire of God's revival.

Bob's foul language stopped immediately after his salvation. His temper came under control. God delivered Him from pornography and other vices. As a wrecker driver, he would occasionally drop by our office in the middle of the day just to say, "I need prayer." Someone would pray with him, then he'd go on his way. After smoking three packs of cigarettes a day for 23 years, Bob started praying about that habit. A year after his conversion, he asked me to anoint him with oil because he believed he was near a breakthrough. Then he quit smoking. Overnight.

That gave Bob the idea that Jesus could intervene with habits his friends were trying to kick in the AA groups. When they asked how he quit, Bob would just say, "Jesus did it." He was a walking miracle who had kicked heroin, methadone and nicotine. He started bringing Jesus into the 12-step group. After Houston Prayer Mountain, he started his own group called "Jesus in the Steps." This program is not a 12-step program but a 14-step program with Jesus as the first and the last step, the Alpha and the Omega, the beginning and the end. Today many such groups are thriving in Houston. Instead of a "higher power," people are learning the truth of who Jesus is.

God wants us to die to our flesh and embrace truth, loving it even more than life itself, because He has more for us. He wants to move through us by His Spirit and bring multitudes into His kingdom. He is preparing hearts now for an outpouring of His Spirit. While some of us will experience a great outpouring of grace and blessing like Bob did, others will experience judgment to deal with compromise and complacency. If our society is going to change, the change must begin with us.

CHAPTER TEN

Therefore let us not sleep, as others do, but let us watch and be sober.

1 THESSALONIANS 5:6

OUR DATE WITH DESTINY

Brenda didn't know a soul when she went. All she knew as a single mom was that a free meal for her four children was too good to pass up, even if it came with some strings attached. Despite her misgivings about using the gasoline, Brenda loaded her children into the old Buick and drove to the "Supper Bowl" in Tampa, Florida, the weekend before the NFL's Super Bowl game. What she received was so much more than a free meal.

Professional athletes encouraged Brenda's children to do well in school and told them it didn't cost a penny to gain self-discipline and learn diligence. Ministers told stories of people who had come up from neighborhoods like hers and built tremendous lives for themselves based on their faith in God. Some workers at the event took an interest in Brenda and told her their church had an outreach for single mothers. For the first time in four years, Brenda felt something so unusual that at first she couldn't figure out what it was. Hope was birthed in her heart that day.

Multiply Brenda's story hundreds of times and you understand the impact Somebody Cares Tampa Bay is making on their community by coordinating with sports teams and Christian athletes. They have evangelized their city with stadium events and created feeding programs in conjunction with the local Devil Rays sports team. They have linked arms with the Book of Hope campaign, helped to facilitate large evangelistic concerts and coordinated with Operation Blessing to conduct school assemblies and massive feedings.

In addition, they hold an annual Compassion Banquet where they invite the media to help them recognize and appreciate the work of dozens of frontline ministries. I was at the kickoff meeting for Somebody Cares Tampa Bay when 100 pastors signed a covenant of unity, Somebody Cares Tampa Bay director Dan Bernard is ensuring that the Brendas of his community receive help to raise their children as productive citizens and have the opportunity to receive Christ as Savior and Lord.

Who Is Our Neighbor?

Fruitful Christians seize opportunities to be Jesus' witnesses. Fruitless Christians squander opportunities. Although we may be believers, failure to take action leaves us powerless and fruitless. True Christianity on the inside, with its corresponding actions, is marked by the power of God. It brings change, ushers in revival and awakens the society around it.

A "certain lawyer" asked Jesus what he must do to inherit eternal life. Since the man knew the Old Testament Scriptures well, Jesus asked him what they said. The lawyer responded, "You shall love the LORD your God with all your heart, with all your soul, with all your strength, and with all your mind, and your neighbor as yourself" (Luke 10:25-37). Jesus told the lawyer that his answer was correct and if he would do this, he would live. The lawyer had all the right words, but Jesus was probing his heart to see if his actions would speak the same message.

We can have the right answer without having a right heart.

Jesus showed that the lawyer was intent only on justifying himself. Instead of being humbled by the requirements of God's law, the man tried to find an escape clause by asking, "Who is my neighbor?"

Jesus wasn't about to let the lawyer wriggle out of his responsibilities. Although the lawyer wanted to pick and choose his neighbors so he could be judged as righteous, Jesus ended the discussion with shocking news: Everyone we encounter is our neighbor!

Jesus then told the story of the Good Samaritan, in which a priest and a Levite passed by a needy person, but a despised Samaritan was the one to stop and help. According to some theologians, the priest who passed by was going to minister in the temple, an honor bestowed on him only once every few years. The priest felt that by helping the wounded man he would miss his opportunity. Yet he failed to recognize that ministry is all about reaching people. By ignoring the man who was bleeding and dying, the priest passed up an opportunity to show love to his neighbor.

A DOER OF THE WORD

In Florida, a man's son was in a hospital, dying of leukemia. One day, while heading to the hospital, the father noticed a homeless boy on the street. The father could have responded like the priest or the Levite because he was already caring for his son. He could have justified ignoring the homeless boy by saying, "I have my own problems; I can't take care of any more."

Yet even with his own son critically ill, the man stopped. He saw an immediate need—a little boy who was homeless, needy and hungry—and that became his immediate calling. He looked beyond his own circumstances and even the needs of his own child to help a homeless stranger. As a result of this man taking the time to help, the boy grew into a young man who now directs a worldwide ministry to children and the homeless.

The Good Samaritan must have had a degree of wealth because he was able to pay for the needy man's hotel and food. Yet even if he had his own business to attend to, when he found a man bleeding and dying on the side of the road he gladly tended to the man's wounds and took him to a place of rest and shelter. This was not goose bumps love—it was love *in action*.

At the end of the story, Jesus turned to the lawyer and said, "Go and do likewise" (Luke 10:37). Like the lawyer, we need to go beyond giving the right answers and the correct theological formulations. We must be "doers of the word, and not hearers only" (Jas. 1:22).

Don't Miss the Green Light

One evening I was driving home late, exhausted and bleary-eyed, anxious to make the last turn and get into my own driveway. As I waited for the left-turn arrow, a carload of people drove up beside me. I looked over at them. They didn't have a green light so they didn't move. I watched them for a moment or two, and as I did, my light turned green, then yellow, then red. When I looked forward again, I had missed the green light!

The next morning I thought about that again and realized that at one time or another each of us misses an opportunity because we get distracted. We can only be His witnesses if we keep our eyes on Him.

In addition to being focused on the Lord, we must be alert for opportunities to minister to those He brings across our path. *If we're looking in the right direction, we will see the light turn green and go!*

A man who responded to the altar call for salvation at Heal Our Land Houston had been in a cult most of his life. Because of a serious accident he was disabled and incapable of working. His girlfriend supported them as a nude dancer. The man asked me in all sincerity, "Doug, what should we do? If she quits her job, that's our only income."

How would you respond? We called on the Lord, and the man and his girlfriend decided she would quit her job, even though they had no idea how they would make a living. We referred them to a church and that following Sunday they attended. During the service, the man was miraculously healed of his disability and was able to go back to work.

The more we become involved in the harvest, the more we are confronted by perplexing situations. Do our words and our testimonies show the love of God? Can people trust us? Do we trust God to solve the world's problems?

The apostle Paul exhorts us to stay awake and alert, remaining watchful and sober lest the day of the Lord overtake us as a thief in the night (see 1 Thess. 5:1-11). The day of the Lord won't overtake us in total surprise if we have watched, prayed and gone about the business of the Lord. We can't know the day or the hour of His coming, but because we're in tune with the Holy Spirit, we can recognize the changing of the seasons.

When Phil and Pam Woods were newly out of college, they came to Houston and helped their youth pastor as youth coordinators at a local church. Phil also got involved with our

Turning Point inner-city ministry on the streets, reaching out to street kids with us. Phil and Pam ended up moving on when Phil received promotions within his company. Today he is an executive for a communications company based in Dallas. He is still highly involved with ministry and he continues to serve on Turning Point's board.

Pam Woods, director of a ministry called Precious Parcels, seized an opportunity that turned into a tremendous ministry of comfort and encouragement for terminally ill children and their parents. After Pam read an article in the December 1998 issue of *Good Housekeeping* magazine about a woman in Oregon who was writing letters and sending Christmas gifts to sick children, she tracked down the woman's phone number. After talking with her, Pam was moved to begin doing something similar in Texas. She contacted us at Turning Point and, after talking with us, knew this idea had a natural home in the Somebody Cares outreach arm. Precious Parcels—a ministry of prayer, letter writing and gift sending to sick children—was born in January 1999.

In the past two years Precious Parcels has mailed 1,089 letters and over 100 Christmas and birthday gifts. It has sponsored events such as the Leukemia Society of America's "Light the Night" Walk and the Dallas White Rock Marathon to benefit a children's hospital in Dallas, where much-needed surgical operations for children are provided at no charge to their families. Many people along the way have donated stickers, stamps, writing materials such as postcards and envelopes, and toys to be used as birthday and Christmas gifts.

A grateful dad wrote, "We can't even begin to tell you how much it means to Nicole (age 11). We tell everyone about Precious Parcels. What means the most to us is the prayers. Without them and God's help we would never make it. All we can say is we love what you do, and thank you."

A mother wrote, "I am Vincent's (age 6) mother and I would like to say thank you for helping him look forward to each day. When I go check the mail he asks me 'Did I receive mail?' He can tell by the stickers on the envelopes which letters are for him. Thank you so much."

Pam Woods remarks, "As with any ministry, there are good days and bad days. Our worst days are when we have to say good-bye to one of these little ones as they go to meet the Lord. We know God has always held them in the palm of his hand and that now they have no sickness and no pain. It is for the families that we grieve and pray. God works all things together for good."

Fruitful or Fruitless?

When we get distracted and fail to seize opportunities to minister to others and to follow closely after Jesus, we can be categorized as having one of three heart conditions depicted in Jesus' parable of the sown seeds (see Luke 8:11-15). One of the most

TO BE FRUITFUL, WE MUST ABIDE IN CHRIST AND ALLOW HIM TO TENDERIZE OUR HEARTS TO THE NEEDS AROUND US.

prevalent attitudes is to become distracted by the cares or the riches and pleasures of life. We can interpret this as getting distracted by the frustrations, disappointments and hurts that occur along life's way instead of maintaining an eternal perspective on life's circumstances and racing on to the finish line.

While people are hungering and thirsting for truth and for answers to life's dilemmas, we have something of substance to offer them, and we will be able to offer it if we keep our eyes on Jesus. If we allow our roots to go deep, we will not be uprooted or fall when the winds of life come or the shaking begins. To be fruitful Christians, we must abide in Christ and allow Him to tenderize our hearts to the needs around us. Let's get ready, for our greatest tests and greatest opportunities are yet to come!

When we exalt Jesus and meditate on His promises, we will overcome all that opposes His will and purpose for our lives. When we hear lies such as, "You have no fight in you, and you will not be able to go another day," we can bring that thought into captivity to the obedience of Christ (see 2 Cor. 10:5). During intense times, victory will only come as we fix our hearts on Jesus.

The Devil Wants Our Right Eye

The devil wants to distract us so that we will miss opportunities and not fulfill our purpose. He wants to divert our focus to the things of this world and take our hearts captive to lust, idolatry, fear, doubt and discouragement. Satan tries to negate the authority we have in Christ by stealing the Word of God out of our hearts and robbing us of the vision God has given us. He wants to stop us from reaching souls, and he wants to destroy us in the process.

In an Old Testament account, the men of Jabesh Gilead feared a ruler named Nahash, whose name means serpent—a clear picture of the devil (see 1 Sam. 11). They desired to make a covenant that would mean their servitude to Nahash but would afford them peaceful coexistence. What a deception to think that we could have peaceful coexistence with the devil, who will only be satisfied with our total humiliation and destruction!

Nahash replied, "On this condition I will make a covenant with you, that I may put out all your right eyes, and bring reproach on all Israel" (1 Sam. 11:2).

The right eye was significant because a soldier took up his shield in his left hand and his sword in his right hand. In order to gauge the enemy's location he would look around the shield with his right eye. Without that eye, the soldier would be totally crippled in his attempt to ward off and conquer the enemy. The same is true in the spiritual realm today. By putting out our right eyes, the devil hopes to disarm us in our efforts to accomplish our commission. If we were to allow Satan to put out our spiritual right eyes, we would be crippled in our ability to attack and destroy his work in people's lives.

The men of Jabesh-Gilead succumbed to the enemy's threats instead of finding encouragement in the Lord and trusting Him. The name Jabesh means "dry." Although these men were no doubt strong warriors, they were dry in their hearts. Because of their dryness in relationship to the Lord, they succumbed to unbelief and discouragement. They lost all desire to fight. Even so, God intervened, and they did not lose their ability to contend with the enemy—they did not lose their right eyes.

God has intervened on our behalf through Jesus Christ (see 2 Cor. 10:5). We, too, can become weary, but we do not have to give place to discouragement and compromise when we have seemingly lost our joy, hope and vision. Scripture reminds us:

> And they overcame him by the blood of the Lamb and by the word of their testimony, and they did not love their lives to the death. Therefore rejoice, O heavens, and you who dwell in them! Woe to the inhabitants of the earth

and the sea! For the devil has come down to you, having great wrath, because he knows that he has a short time (Rev. 12:11,12).

MAKE JESUS "THE MAN"

God wants His people to be victorious, but sometimes we don't know how. In 1998, I was invited to be the keynote speaker for a conference hosted by Gary Ham of Operation Breaking Through in Virginia Beach, Virginia. The conference was kicked off by a citywide prayer breakfast during which Reggie White spoke. Several years earlier, the Green Bay Packers football team had signed Reggie, and many people openly predicted that he would lead the team to the Super Bowl.

Upon arriving to meet his new team, Reggie told them what it would take to get to the Super Bowl and to become world champions. He said, "There's something we need to understand. It's not about me, it's not about you; it's about making Brett Favre 'the man.'" Reggie said they needed to protect quarterback Favre and help him be a success. In so doing, the whole team would be a success.

That principle is the key to fulfilling our mission as the Church: It's not about you, and it's not about me. It's about making Jesus "the Man." In other words, it's not about your ministry or mine, your denomination or mine; it's about lifting up the name of Jesus and extending His Lordship across the earth. When He is glorified, we as His Church are successful in our calling. But when we pursue our own interests, the whole team fails.

The Green Bay Packers did become Super Bowl champs. Who got to share in the team's victory? Reggie, Brett and everyone associated with the Packers organization—coaches, trainers, people in the front office and in less visible areas of the organization.

The whole team benefits when each member becomes content with the position he has been given. When a person is discontent and tries to fill someone else's position, the whole team suffers. To become part of a winning team, everyone in the Green Bay Packers organization recognized that, individually, they must commit to something bigger than themselves.

When Reggie speaks to ministers, he often points out that they will never fulfill their destiny unless they operate as a T.E.A.M., meaning Together Everyone Achieves More. Whether in sports or in the Body of Christ, this principle is crucial to realizing our full effectiveness.

THE EDGE OF ETERNITY

When we work as a team—seeing our call to become part of something bigger than ourselves—and our hearts are prepared by remaining focused on the Lord and on souls, no catastrophic national or international event will come upon us unaware. We will not be stumped by any perplexing moral dilemma. We will not lose our "right eye" ability to fight the devil, nor will we be moved from our place of relationship with the Lord and His calling.

Throughout history, in times of peace and prosperity, we as the Church have tended to compromise and become divided, concerned mostly with building our own kingdoms. We have been united mostly in times of poverty and persecution—and that is when revival has most often come. God wants to get our attention *now*. He wants us to be united in our efforts *now*.

I see that happening more and more. In Denver, Colorado, pastors and ministry leaders are coordinating Somebody Cares Denver by identifying what pastors and ministries are already doing in that city. They have already sponsored marches with benevolence and outreach. Somebody Cares Southland in California is helping to feed as many as 90,000 people monthly through the united efforts of people like servant director Norm Brinkley, Indonesia Relief Fund founder and leader Paul Tan and many others. Others have taken the DNA of this ministry, and the concept is going forward in other countries.

Combined effort unites us as people and causes us to care for others more deeply than casual awareness allows. Uniting our efforts also creates surprising connections. One young Christian named Wendell often went to the streets with me. Bald from chemotherapy, Wendell unashamedly walked the streets to testify of Christ's love in an effort to take as many people as possible to heaven with him. Wendell eventually died from the cancer. Some time later, as Wendell's parents worked through their grief, they were asked to give someone a ride to church. They asked the young woman how she had come to know Christ. "I was out on the streets," came the reply, "and someone named Wendell and someone named Doug told me about Jesus."

Leonard Ravenhill once wrote a note to me that said, "Let others live on the raw edge or the cutting edge. You and I should live on the edge of eternity." How can we settle into complacency while multitudes upon multitudes hang in the balance of eternity? How can we be so hard of heart as to sit back on the beach of comfort and apathy while so many are still shipwrecked in the sea of death? How can we fight one another when the world needs us to come together with one purpose—to win souls to Christ? We have been called for such a time as this, and we must not miss our date with destiny.

CHAPTER ELEVEN

And the Spirit and the bride say, "Come!" And let him who hears say, "Come!" And let him who thirsts come. Whoever desires, let him take the water of life freely.

REVELATION 22:17

THE NET THAT WORKS

During a street interview with a 14-year-old many years ago, the young teen said with an air of pride, "I'm a prostitute. That's all I know." Yet underneath that callous exterior was a little girl crying out for love. Brandy was her name. She gave birth to and gave away at least a couple of children that we know of during the time we worked with her.

We consistently reached out to Brandy, making sure she had our Somebody Cares business card with the telephone number. We would hear from her for a while and then there were long periods with no contact. All the same, she gave us the opportunity to give her the gospel and plant seeds of love in her heart.

Regardless of where Brandy lived or what she did for a living, she knew someone cared for her, and we knew Someone besides us had His eye on her.

Thirteen years after we met Brandy, she contracted the AIDS virus. On a chilly Friday morning in April 2000, a longtime Turning Pointer, Susie Wolf, pulled into the parking lot of our offices. Jen, a young prostitute, was standing there waiting and crying. As Susie approached her, Jen said, "Brandy's dead."

The shock was almost too much for Susie. So often when Brandy had called, Susie and other Turning Pointers had gone to her aid. Even though she was in and out of jail for various charges, no one ever doubted that in the end Brandy's life would be claimed for the kingdom of God. As Susie pieced together what had happened, she found that after Brandy's last release from jail she had gone to an AIDS hospice. She was incoherent at the end, yet we trust the seeds of truth planted throughout the years took root, and Brandy cried out to Jesus for life.

CASTING THE NET

When we pour ourselves into the lives of people, each person has a choice to either reject or accept our help and our Jesus. Hollywood was an older street kid who pimped out street girls for a living. We saw him often, witnessed to him and even got him to pray the sinner's prayer. But he never came off the streets, and that's where he died of a gunshot wound to the head. Derrah, who ran with Hollywood, heard our witness but ended up in jail for drugs.

Shawn prostituted herself to make a living. Opey was seduced by homosexuals to sell his body for food because he was starving to death. He was hooked on heavy metal music and needed deliverance. Michael bit through his tongue in a car accident and couldn't speak well because he constantly drooled. Although he was a nice kid, he was perceived as crazy because of his appearance, so he lived the part. Icepick was a crackhead and pimp who came off the streets, but only for a time.

Kevin went to live with a minister in another state after he broke out of the New Age movement. He was delivered of his music addiction when he literally broke in two a guitar given to him by a warlock. Diana was a lesbian who saw gay men being saved and followed their path to the altar, which radically changed and freed her. Regina's car was parked outside a topless bar where she worked. Leaving work one night, she found a tract left on her car and decided maybe there was hope for her. She called the number and committed her life to Christ.

Fear of others' rejection is no reason to allow hell to claim their lives. We must continue to reach out to them.

COSMETIC CHRISTIANITY

It's easy to say what the people described in the previous paragraphs needed to do—they needed to leave their lifestyles behind. But is it as obvious to know what we must do? Are there struggles or sins in our lives that hinder us from reaching out to others? Are we holding out on God?

Cosmetic Christianity is a plague within the Body of Christ. It is a spirituality that is superficial and only skin-deep. Like the parable of the barren fig tree, it promotes leaves—the appearance of spirituality—but it fails to produce the fruit and the character of Christ. Some cosmetic Christians actually have a relationship with the Lord, but some serious pruning is needed in their lives.

We are entering a season when we can no longer get away with things that are not pleasing to God. *Anything in our lives that is not like Christ must go!*

Even as Christians, we may try to cover up our hurts, fears, insecurities and weaknesses through various kinds of compensatory façades. Such masks are an attempt to compensate on the outside for something we lack on the inside. The façade can be something "spiritual" such as Christian service. Or it can be a worldly cover-up such as drugs, alcohol, promiscuity, gang activity or even material success. Whether the mask is spiritual or worldly, it will prove futile in bringing true fulfillment. Our freedom comes only as we are open and transparent before the Lord.

Digging Out the Rocks

Several years ago some Turning Pointers and I served on a missions team in Central America. We were helping a Youth With A Mission (YWAM) base that was working in a local village. One of our assignments was to help dig an outhouse hole. I dug several feet down and hit a boulder. I soon realized that I could not get past this large rock, hard as I tried. The only way I could remove the boulder was to dig around it until I could get leverage to hoist it out of the hole.

Through that arduous process, the Lord spoke to my heart. Often our hearts contain hard rocks or boulders that block our spiritual progress. The Lord has to dig in our hearts, chipping away at any areas of hardness to pull out those boulders. There is no shame in willingly exposing ourselves before the Lord, because He knows and cares for us.

The enemy is cunning, and he knows how to appeal to our flesh. His tactics are no different today than the ones he used on Adam and Eve in the Garden. "For God knows that in the day you eat of it [the forbidden fruit] your eyes will be opened, and you will be like God, knowing good and evil" (Gen. 3:5). By such enticing words, the enemy tries to draw us into his web. His temptation looks good and seems pleasant and desirable. Why is it that our human nature always seems to want what it cannot have? This was the initial temptation presented to Adam and Eve.

As soon as they ate from the tree, their eyes were opened. They now saw things from the world's standards. In the Garden, Adam and Eve had the peace that passes understanding, joy unspeakable and everything good. The only thing they lacked or had to gain was evil. Yet the very thing they did not have, they desired.

When we believe the lies of the enemy that we *must be something* we are not, or *have something* we don't, we are no longer content being who we are in Christ. Believing a lie brings shame, and in our distress, rather than running *to* the Lord, we run *from* Him.

Transparent Before the Lord and Each Other

After eating the forbidden fruit, Adam and Eve experienced shame so they covered themselves and hid. "Then the eyes of both of them were opened, and they knew that they were naked; and they sewed fig leaves together and made themselves coverings." The Lord then asked Adam, "Where are you?" Adam answered, "I was afraid because I was naked; and I hid myself" (see Gen. 3:7-10).

Who told Adam he was naked? Who told you that you were naked? Who brings shame, fear of rejection and lies into our lives? What standard have we set for ourselves other than God's truth?

Being open and totally transparent before the Lord was Adam and Eve's original state and it is our opportunity today. God knows everything about us already, so there is nothing to fear. We may be tempted by things in this world that seem good and pleasant, but if those things become our standard, we will no longer have peace in being transparent before the Lord.

God wants us to look to Him and be content in Him. Our standard must be based on His purity, holiness and righteousness—even though we don't think we can fit this standard. *It's better to try to fit His standards than to bring His standards down to ours.*

This generation wants what is real and they are examining our lifestyle to see if we are authentic. We must allow the Lord access to those places of our hearts that we've hidden from Him. He wants only our good, because He loves us. We lost our innocence in the Garden, but Jesus gave it back at the cross! That is our hope and our victory.

Being right with God comes with the price of our willingness to take off the masks, remove the façades and cover-ups and let Him do a work inside us. God is not looking for those who merely *look like* Christians, He is looking for those who are the real deal. He wants believers who are the same inside and out. When we are transparent before the Lord, His light shines upon us and we radiate the very character and nature of His Son. That is what He is looking for and what the world hopes we have to offer—truth, honesty and brokenness.

HUNGER FOR HOLINESS

Revival and holiness are synonymous. Revival is always first a revival of holiness and consecration. God is depositing a depth of character and a hunger for His holiness in each one of us who seek Him. As one Youth With a Mission leader stated about the Lord's work in Houston, "It is a revival of character."

The Lord wants to build a depth of character in our lives so that the move of His Spirit among us is not shallow and narrow, but deep and wide. For that to happen we have to allow the Lord to uproot the old so that we can put on the new. When Jesus told His disciples that a grain seed had to die in order to bear fruit, He was speaking about Himself and us as well (see John 12:24).

During the Passover season of Bible times, the priest would take grains of wheat and scatter them in a field outside the city. He would then come back into the temple and sacrifice a lamb for the Passover. A pivotal year in history came when Jesus and the Passover lamb of the temple were sacrificed at the same time. On the following Sunday morning before sunrise, the priest who had scattered the grains of wheat went out to see if they had sprouted. If so, he pulled up a few of the sprouts. He then brought those sprouts—the firstfruits—into the temple and offered them on the altar.

At the same time as the sprouts were offered, Jesus, the first fruit of the resurrection, arose. The grain of wheat had gone into the ground and died. Jesus had been buried, but on the third day He arose.

Every time we make a sacrifice for His kingdom, we die to the flesh and God is glorified. From that place of sacrifice and death comes great fruitfulness and harvest. Death to self results in resurrection and multiplication. From our sacrifice, God will raise up what He desires in our lives. Though we may think we have little to offer, if we will offer ourselves, the Lord will produce a surprising fruitfulness. Jesus is returning for a Church that has sown her life into the lives of others.

CAN WE HEAR THEM?

One day recently as I met with a pastor and his wife, my cell phone rang. They waited politely, assuming that I was talking with my office or some minister.

When I ended the call, the pastor asked, "Doug, who was that?"

"A crack addict," I replied. "He just needed some encouragement on how to seek the Lord. He hasn't broken his addiction yet, but I believe he's going to make it."

They sat quietly for a moment; then, teary-eyed, his wife spoke. "Your heart has never changed," she said. "You still take the time to minister one-on-one. It's the same core DNA as you had back at that apartment years ago when you were trusting God for a bag of groceries."

MAKING AN IMPACT ON THE WORLD IS ALL ABOUT MEETING REAL PEOPLE, WHO HAVE REAL NEEDS, WITH THE REALITY OF JESUS.

Let us never arrive at a point where we no longer hear the cries of people's hearts. Let us not be so caught up in church life with the masses that we no longer have time for individuals ravaged by sin. Let's stop being in such a hurry to get to a choir practice or a prayer meeting that we pass all the needy on the street without so much as a whispered prayer for them.

An alarm is going off around the world. It's time for the Church to arise and beckon people to enter the Kingdom. We have been sent on a rescue mission to the multitudes by becoming a mended net cast into the waters to bring in a mighty harvest of souls.

Some say they want to impact the world, but they never seem to get started. Others claim that the challenges are just too great.

Making an impact is actually a fairly simple task. *It's all about meeting real people, who have real needs, with the reality of Jesus.*

SOULS AT THE CROSSROADS

The life of Brandy, the young prostitute mentioned at the beginning of this chapter, illustrates the crossroads faced by every lost person today. Who will point them to Christ? Who will patiently help them, instruct them and plant in them seeds of eternal life?

Even though Turning Pointers worked with Brandy for years, she continued to struggle with her sinful lifestyle, ultimately dying of AIDS. Susie Wolf called all over the city the day Brandy died but could not locate a single person who would claim to be related to the girl. Without next of kin, the county would have no recourse but to bury Brandy as an indigent in a pauper's grave. But Brandy did have family. She had us. We would claim Brandy. We would mourn for her as one of our own. After a series of calls were made, I discovered that we could claim Brandy and give her a proper funeral for $2,500. I quickly gathered a small group of Turning Pointers and together we viewed a brief video clip of Brandy. Everyone agreed to help.

On the day of the funeral, local ministers, including Fred Forshag, George Matranga, Henry Dibrell and Mark LeCrone, assisted with the service. Mark now pastors a church in the Lower Westheimer area where we first met Brandy.

The local news media heard what we were doing and came out to ask why. At the service, topless dancers, street kids and AIDS victims mixed with hospice workers and Turning Pointers. A young man we've known for over 15 years had lived on the streets at the same time as Brandy. They stayed up many nights talking about their lives until he left the streets and entered a men's discipleship program. He said that Brandy was "a big sister who looked out for me. She even took the blame for some things I did out there."

Brandy touched many lives. Lori, whom I'd met years earlier as she stood over her children's stroller while waiting to turn a trick, attended. She, too, now has AIDS. During the service she shared a few words about Brandy, then turned and pointed at me and said, "I wish I'd never left. I wish I'd listened to you back then."

What will the people of your city say as they point a finger at you? Will they say they wished they had listened or will they ask why you never told them? Each of us is vital to the lives of those we meet. We could be the only family others will ever know. There *is* hope for the world. There is hope for young men and women just like Brandy out on the streets today. Their hope is found in you and me. We are a tangible expression of Jesus' love for them.

The apostle Paul was often rejected, even persecuted and beaten, yet he helped win to Christ almost half the known world of his day. Listen to his joy at the work God did in his converts at Thessalonica: "What is our hope, or joy, or crown of rejoicing? Is it not even you in the presence of our Lord Jesus Christ at His coming? For you are our glory and joy" (1 Thess. 2:19,20).

This same joy can be ours as we unite to reach out to lost and hurting people with the power of the gospel. Will we continue on the road of complacency or press on down the road toward revival? Will we build our own kingdoms or join together to build God's kingdom? Never before have we been given such incredible opportunities to reach our cities for Christ. We have this amazing hour in which to fulfill our destiny. We must let nothing deter, distract or discourage us. We must act now.

IS THE SAFETY NET READY?

When I think of all the people whose souls are hanging in the balance of an eternity without God, I am reminded of the tragic story of the *Titanic*. In stark contrast to Noah, who by divine warning obeyed God and built a ship (ark) for the saving of his family (see Genesis 6-9), those who worked with the *Titanic* arrogantly said that even God Himself couldn't sink her.

There were six warnings sent to the *Titanic* prior to when she hit the iceberg that sank her. Throughout the day, various ships, such as the *Californian* and the *Carpathia,* sent warnings of impending danger; yet all warnings were scorned, and the rest is history.

We can see a parallel between the fate of the *Titanic* and the fate of a people who choose to ignore God's warnings. The word "pride" could be used to describe the actions of the crew of the *Titanic,* as pride can describe so many today who reject the warnings of the Lord. But there were also three other ships in the *Titanic* story that must not be overlooked.

The *Samson* was a ship that many did not hear about until years later. The *Samson* was the closest ship to the sinking *Titanic* and could have aided in rescuing many of those who perished in the icy sea, yet it chose to leave the scene. The crew of the *Samson* was involved in the illegal hunting of seals, and because they were afraid of getting caught, they turned off their lights and sailed away, leaving hundreds to die a horrific death. How many professing Christians have rendered themselves ineffective in rescuing perishing souls? Due to the dark deeds of sin, some do nothing. They run away from, rather than toward, those who are shipwrecked in the sea of death.

The next closest ship, the *Californian,* was approximately seventeen to eighteen miles away from the distress call of the *Titanic.* Earlier, the *Californian* had sent warnings to the *Titanic* about the danger of icebergs, only to be ignored. Although the *Californian* was only a few miles away, they slowly and cautiously proceeded toward the sinking *Titanic,* fearing for their own safety. There may have been a bit of pride involved in their decision not to hasten. After all, they did try to warn the *Titanic.* I wonder how many believers choose to do nothing to help rescue the perishing because they don't want to risk their own discomfort?

The third ship, the *Carpathia,* was nearly forty-eight miles away from the *Titanic.* But when they received the distress call, they immediately chose to go full speed ahead. They, too, had earlier warned the *Titanic,* and their warnings went unheeded. The fog was thick, making it very dangerous for them to maneuver past icebergs. At the risk of their own lives and against all odds, the *Carpathia* chose to rescue the perishing. They were able to save the lives of just over 700 people, while hundreds of others were buried in an icy grave. How many more could have been rescued had the *Samson* and the *Californian* assisted the rescue efforts?

Like the passengers on the *Titanic,* people today are cruising along in smug complacency, living in relative prosperity. But when calamity comes, will there be adequate lifeboats to handle shipwrecked victims?

The Church needs to prepare for such a day. Mending our nets is not just a nice idea to make us look spiritual; it is a matter of life and death to the countless people who will drown when their lives strike an unexpected iceberg. In that day the mended net will be a safety net to rescue lives for the Kingdom.

If our government welfare net were to rip open, would the Church be ready to provide a network of food and clothing distribution to accommodate millions of people as we did in previous decades before government welfare? The answer is yes if the Church unites now. By uniting in a similar way to the Somebody Cares network, we can position ourselves and prepare for the latter rain, the shaking and the fires of revival. The fire will burn, the wind will blow and the rain will fall, but the effect they have on us individually and corporately will depend on what we have done to prepare.

DEEP AND WIDE

Prior to the 2000 presidential election, I was asked to speak at a large political convention. I would have spoken the same words regardless of which political party I was addressing. Little did I realize those words would resound and reverberate across America in what I believe is a prophetic word to the nation.

The following paragraphs, ending in a prayer modeled after a passage from Isaiah 37:15-20, are the gist of what I said that day.

Everywhere I go today I hear young people say, "Give me something to believe in." Hundreds of years ago, Hezekiah, a great national leader, said, "This day is a day of trouble and rebuke and blasphemy; for the children have come to birth, but there is no strength to bring them forth" (Isa. 37:3). Today's generation of young people are looking for something to believe in. They are ready to be released into their destiny, but they need hope to bring that destiny to life. What we need in America again is hope.

My prayer and my heart's cry is that our words would come from the innermost part of our hearts and not be just shallow platitudes or façades that compensate for a lack on the inside. I pray that we would help give strength to this generation that is ready to put their hope in something. They need to see a revival of character. They need to see a revival of trust in those who say they are leading them into the next century—the next millennium. . . .

My prayer is that America would be a nation of hope once again . . . a nation of character . . . a nation in which all people can trust us. . . . a nation in which this young generation will find their hope again and the outcast, the lame and the sick will be a strong nation.

Lord God, You alone are God. Incline your ear to hear and open your eyes to see the distress and trouble, despair and hopelessness we see in the inner cities of America and all across this nation and around the world. We recognize that our shallow words and platitudes and our own efforts alone cannot bring change. We need your intervention. We need a revival of character. . . .
Give a release to this young generation looking for something to believe in. Give them hope again. And, Father, release them to their destiny to walk in character, integrity and in the hope that they would lead us across the Jordan to a place of promise where the world can look to us and say they want some of that. Incline your ear, O Lord, and hear. Open Your eyes, O Lord, and see. Intervene on our behalf and make us a great nation again. In Jesus' name. Amen.

To the Ends of the Earth

When we see that what God has called us to do is too big for us, we will finally be ready for God to use us. Pastor Paul Tan, serving with Somebody Cares Southland (in California) was feeling overwhelmed one day as he considered the huge responsibility of reaching cities for Christ. As he cried out to the Lord, Paul sensed the Lord saying, "If it's not too big for you, then you don't need Me!" Indeed, God will never give us a mission that we can accomplish without His help or the help of our brothers and sisters.

When we come together, seeking God's strategy and power, there will be amazing fruit. Onlookers will see something we never could have accomplished without the Lord and each other.

"In Jerusalem, and in all Judea and Samaria, and to the end of the earth" (Acts 1:8). This is a blueprint for any ministry vision. We first reach our local communities, our "Jerusalem." Then we reach other parts of the nation, our "Judea." From there we take the Kingdom to neighboring countries and throughout the world, our "Samaria" and "the ends of the earth." The same Kingdom principles work everywhere.

As we faithfully follow the Lord, our fig trees will be full. Our nets will bring in a great catch without breaking. It is harvest-time, and from every seed that dies we can expect a great crop. Many will be brought out of the valley of decision because true witnesses will have rescued their lives.

Just as the owner of the vineyard gave the keeper a season to nurture the tree, we have been given a window of opportunity to fulfill God's purposes for this generation. The darkness is growing darker and the light is getting lighter: "Where sin abounded, grace abounded much more" (Rom. 5:20). Together we must commit ourselves to His purpose and prepare people for His coming. This is our privilege and our calling.

To start Somebody Cares in your city is easier
than you think! Contact:

Somebody Cares
P.O. Box 570007
Houston, Texas 77257-0007

(713) 621-1498
www.somebodycares.org

"A true witness rescues lives" (Prov. 14:25).